Praise for

WHAT THEY MEANT FOR EVIL

"Rebecca's story brings the real-life experiences of a courageous refugee to life. The beauty of her homeland, the heartache of loss, the trauma of abuse and war, and the joy of new beginnings. I pray that Rebecca's story will help all of us understand in new ways the plight of the sixty-five million refugees around the world, and how God's love—and God's Word of hope—can transform lives for His glory."

—Dr. Roy L. Peterson, president and CEO of
American Bible Society

"When you meet the vibrant, joy-filled, and engaging Rebecca Deng, you'd never know the horrors of what she had to deal with and overcome at such a young age. Surviving in a war-torn country, traveling over miles of rough terrain— often by foot—to get to what she believed would be safety, only to discover more tragedy. But through it all, Rebecca found a strength and bravery to combat the worst levels of trauma and come out victorious, healthy, and whole. In WHAT THEY MEANT FOR EVIL, Rebecca shares a page-turning account of the raw realities of evil but also the overcoming power of faith and bravery. This is a must-read for anyone who wants to make a real difference in the world."

—Kirk Cousins, NFL quarterback for the
Minnesota Vikings

"Anyone who wants to understand Khartoum's systematic campaign of genocide, which led to two million deaths in South Sudan—and which continues today to claim countless innocent lives—needs to read Rebecca Deng's story. It is a powerful indictment of a regime that has ruthlessly crucified its Christian people, but it is also a moving and inspiring story of the triumph, in one exceptional life, of love over hate, life over death. It's a story that deserves to be widely known."
—Lord David Alton, former Liberal Democrat Member of Parliament, permanent member of the House of Lords, and cofounder of Chance for Childhood

"In WHAT THEY MEANT FOR EVIL, Deng paints a vivid portrait of her idyllic childhood in a village in South Sudan until her innocence is stolen on a rainy day when soldiers attack her home. The fact that Deng survived her ordeal is, in itself, nothing short of a miracle. That she went on to become an international speaker, author, and vocal advocate for women and children is a testament to her strength of character and faithfulness to God's call. This book is beautifully written and deeply moving. [For me] as president of the Lutheran Immigration and Refugee Service, Deng's incredible story of hope, perseverance, healing, and faith is a very personal reminder of why we are called upon to do this work."
—Linda Hartke, president and CEO of Lutheran Immigration and Refugee Service

"In her stunning memoir WHAT THEY MEANT FOR EVIL, Rebecca Deng tells the story that needs to be heard. Until there is no more war, all stories of war are important. But all too seldom do we hear from the innocents, the 'collateral damage,' the women and the children. Rebecca lost her home and family to violence in South Sudan as a small child, but she faced the struggles of a young woman unprotected in the refugee camp. One of only a handful of Lost Girls, she came to America and made an amazing life for herself and her family. Her strength and spirit shine through. Rebecca's is a voice we need to hear."

—Judy A. Bernstein, coauthor of
They Poured Fire On Us From the Sky:
The True Story of Three Lost Boys of Sudan

"This heart-touching story of Rebecca Deng isn't just another reflection of what happened and is still going on in South Sudan. When reading her story it is like being present at the scene. More than once I found it breathtaking and more than ever before I was motivated to work hard to restore or finally establish peace in South Sudan. A must-read for everyone interested in the reality of what happens in the life of innocent people facing war."

—Henk F. Koppelaar, CEO of
Quintessence, an independent
Dutch consultancy for charities and NGOs

"Do not go through this book; let it go through you!

"You will understand the devastating impact of war and conflict through the raw, authentic voice of a little girl on the run. A little girl growing up in a crowded, poverty-stricken refugee camp, a fifteen-year-old girl forced into motherhood. In her struggles with premature motherhood you will encounter the foster family and the community that welcomed her in Holland, Michigan, and who shaped who she is today.

"Rebecca's story peels the linguistic camouflage used by governments and the media to hide the horrible and brutal impact of war on children. In a world where 'refugees' are a lucrative fund-raising cause, Rebecca is the human being the many fund-raisers' appeals refer to only as nameless refugee children, statistics, and percentages.

"While conventional language defines refugee children as 'broken and helpless,' this is a story of one such child who, with inner strength and support from those who *chose* to care about her, refuses to allow the brokenness to define her future.

"Rebecca refuses to be '*the Lost Girl of South Sudan,*' as the lucky few refugee children from her war-torn country were introduced to America. Rebecca is not the Lost Girl of South Sudan—she is alive and engaged through her story in this book. She defies the helpless victimhood label; she is a thriving overcomer."

—Jane Wathome, director of Global Scripture
Impact at American Bible Society

"No life is lived without hardship. Most of us seek pleasure, not pain, even though we know the travails of life are what test us, build character, create new paths of resiliency, and make it possible to savor the joys and blessings of friendship and family. Rebecca Deng's story is our story. It is about the journey of humanity toward the greater good, a journey that can only happen when each of us makes it happen in our own lives."

—Jonathan C. Lewis, author of
The Unfinished Social Entrepreneur

"Rebecca Deng and Ginger Kolbaba tell an inspiring story of loss, resilience, and faith. The story is based on real-life events of Rebecca Deng during the second Sudanese civil war. In the blaze of destruction and death, Deng was left without a home and her immediate family. Losing the life she knew at the young age of six, her situation propelled her to grow up and keep moving forward. She experienced severe depression and had difficulty coping with her life. Deng looked to faith and education as escape from the horrors of the war and the refugee camps. Her life truly changed when she was granted refugee status in the United States, which gave her the opportunity to begin a new life, study, and become an advocate for peace and change. Deng embodies strength and hope that resounds with the reader in her thrilling story of a lost child from a war-torn country."

—Goran Debelnogich, senior principal analyst,
US Department of Health and Human Services

"With a clear, beautiful, faith-filled voice, Rebecca Deng tells an important and gripping story. Most of us in the West cannot comprehend how life could change so quickly from one of innocence and peace and abundance to such raging evil. But in the life of this former Lost Girl, we see a testimony to the strength and resilience of the people of South Sudan and how they overcame—and continue to overcome—overwhelming challenges and sorrows in their determination to be the country that God created them to be."

—Faith McDonnell, director of the
Religious Liberty Program and
the Church Alliance for a New Sudan,
Institute on Religion and Democracy

"Rebecca was four when enemy soldiers arrived in her village, forcing her to flee and stealing the safety and comfort from her childhood. WHAT THEY MEANT FOR EVIL is the hauntingly beautiful story of Rebecca's experience as she describes the beauty of African life and the horrors and brutality of civil war. Rebecca's story is gripping and sad, but also one of courage and hope as she shares the events that found her walking miles across her country to the promise of safety in a refugee camp and ultimately the promise of a new life in the United States. WHAT THEY MEANT FOR EVIL is an amazing, true story of one of the 'Lost Girls' of Sudan. You will be inspired by Rebecca's determination to hold on to her faith and seek a brighter future for herself and, eventually, to help others traumatized by war to do the same."

—Kathleen Davis VanTol, PhD, associate professor of
education at Dordt College

"Rebecca's contribution to the global refugee crisis conversation is an important one. In a world polarized by extremism, her story invites us into something personal, something tragic and still beautiful, despairing and still hopeful. Her story needs to be shared."

—Jon Brown, pastor of Pillar Church,
Holland, Michigan

"In WHAT THEY MEANT FOR EVIL, Rebecca invites readers to journey with her from her peaceful, playful childhood in South Sudan, through the terrors of war she witnessed while running for her life, to Kakuma Refugee Camp in Northern Kenya, where she found rest from war but trials of a different kind.

"Surviving circumstances and difficulties that require courage to tell, Rebecca moved as a young teenager to the United States, where she managed to navigate a strange, new world and start on a road to personal healing that would change not only her own life, but the lives of countless others around the world.

"While unimaginable to most and unique to her, Rebecca's story speaks to the heart of every reader, no matter their walk or circumstance in life. Rebecca reminds us that, in each and every one of us, there exists the possibility of finding beauty in the ashes of our own struggles, and restoring to wholeness what has been shattered in the lives of those around us. Rebecca's story encourages us that God's plan has always been to take what was broken, wounded, and hurting and make it into something beautiful—in His time and way— for the good of His people and for the glory of His Name."

—Karen Genzink, lead consultant, Asia,
at Whitten & Roy Partnership

"It is such a privilege and I feel so humbled to endorse Rebecca Deng's book of her life. She is an amazing woman! This is her story of how she and many other 'lost' South Sudan boys and girls were persecuted as very young children. It was her faith in God and the love of fellow Christians that kept her strong throughout her incredible journey. Thank You, Jesus, for keeping Your promise of never leaving or forsaking her and using her for Your glory today."

—Elsa Prince-Broekhuizen, philanthropist

"Rebecca's decision to share her story with us, and the grace, redemption, and resilience her life represents, exemplifies God's admonition to us all to 'be strong and courageous…for the Lord your God will be with you wherever you go' (Joshua 1:9). Despite severe and prolonged trauma, she chose not to go through life as a victim but instead to be an agent of hope for Christ and His Kingdom, trusting that the Word of God, the people of God, and the Spirit of God would meet her needs. The manner in which the Lord has blessed her faith and diligence is a wonderful reminder to us all as we deal with the brokenness of life all around us that the Lord has a plan for each of us, 'Plans to prosper you, plans to give you a hope and a future' (Jeremiah 29:11). Thank you, Rebecca, for the gift your story will be for many."

—Samuel A. Beals, chief executive officer, Samaritas

WHAT THEY
MEANT FOR EVIL

WHAT THEY MEANT FOR EVIL

How a Lost Girl of Sudan
Found Healing, Peace, and
Purpose in the Midst of Suffering

REBECCA DENG

with **Ginger Kolbaba**

New York   Nashville

FaithWords
Hachette Book Group
1290 Avenue of the Americas, New York, NY 10104
faithwords.com
twitter.com/faithwords

First Edition: September 2019

FaithWords is a division of Hachette Book Group, Inc. The FaithWords name and logo are trademarks of Hachette Book Group, Inc.

The publisher is not responsible for websites (or their content) that are not owned by the publisher.

The Hachette Speakers Bureau provides a wide range of authors for speaking events. To find out more, go to www.hachettespeakersbureau.com or call (866) 376-6591.

Library of Congress Cataloging-in-Publication Data

Names: Deng, Rebecca, author. | Kolbaba, Ginger, author.
Title: What they meant for evil : how a lost girl of Sudan found healing, peace, and purpose in the midst of suffering / Rebecca Deng with Ginger Kolbaba.
Description: New York : FaithWords, [2019]
Identifiers: LCCN 2018057660 | ISBN 9781546013204 (trade pbk.) | ISBN 9781546013211 (ebook)
Subjects: LCSH: Deng, Rebecca. | Christian biography—Sudan. | Christian biography—United States. | Refugee children—Sudan—Biography. | Sudan—History—Civil War, 1983–2005—Personal narratives. | Sudan—History—Civil War, 1983–2005—Children—Biography. | Sudan—History—Civil War, 1983–2005—Refugees—Biography.
Classification: LCC BR1725.D435 A3 2019 | DDC 276.24/083092 [B]—dc23
LC record available at https://lccn.loc.gov/2018057660

ISBNs: 978-1-5460-1722-6 (hardcover), 978-1-5460-1321-1 (ebook)

Printed in the United States of America

LSC-C

10 9 8 7 6 5 4 3 2 1

This book is dedicated to my firstborn, Achol (Cholie).
You've taught me about beauty, about what it means to be
a mother, and about who I really am.

Contents

Contents

A LOST GIRL

My name is Rebecca Ajueny Nyanwut de Deng de Awel. If I were introducing myself in South Sudan, I would start with my dad's side of the family—Rebecca Ajueny Nyanwut de Deng de Awel de Luk de Ajang de Padict de Ajang. Then I would go on to list my mother's side—Ajueny Nyanwut de Achol de Riak de Gong de Lual de Akau. My name is long because our tradition dictates that we say our name to at least the tenth generation. Growing up, I learned the names of my ancestors to the fifteenth generation, but now I struggle to remember some of them. I was born into the Hol clan of the Dinka tribe. I come from the Pathiel line in a subclan called Pan-Aluk. And I am from the house of Ajang, Pan-Awel Luk. That's a lot to remember!

I am from the village of Aruai Mayen in the Duk Padiet region, which is on the border of Dinka and Nuer land and is located in Sudd, a huge swampland. The village was in Jonglei state in what is now South Sudan, although now it has vanished.

I survived the Bor Massacre of 1991, which completely

wiped out my village, killed thousands of people in one attack, and displaced one hundred thousand. The Sudanese civil war killed roughly two million people and displaced four million. I was one of those displaced.

I am one of the Lost Girls of South Sudan. I am not the first or the last Lost Girl. Much has been told of the forty thousand Lost Boys who were orphaned and fled the country on foot to Ethiopia or served as child soldiers, and of the 3,700 Lost Boys who came to the United States as refugees. Few stories have come out about the eighty-nine Lost Girls who found their way from Kakuma Refugee Camp to the United States. There are many reasons why so few girls made it out of Sudan or the refugee camps. Some were either killed, married off at the tender ages of fifteen or younger, sold as slaves, or are still living in a refugee camp, with little hope for a brighter future. That was what war did to the tens of thousands of innocent children who lost everything—it took their childhood, their innocence, their families, their homes, even their lives.

Leon Trotsky once reportedly said, "You may not be interested in war, but war is interested in you." War is ugly. If people were truly aware of the consequences it inflicts on humanity, no one would ever think of starting it. Now, only those who have borne witness to the destruction of war can attest to its unreversed damages. I have experienced its ruthlessness, how it destroys human dignity and the human spirit.

Yet in the midst of war, of devastating loss, I experienced something unexpected. My life has been one of experiencing grace upon grace. God walked patiently with me through the darkest days to show me that I am his child and that he cares about me, although I didn't always see it clearly. It's difficult to see clearly through pain and trauma.

I do not understand the suffering of the innocent or why the unjust seem to thrive. I have often prayed the prayer of the Old Testament prophet Habakkuk: "Why do you make me see iniquity, and why do you idly look at wrong? Destruction and violence are before me; strife and contention arise" (Habakkuk 1:3).

But even in the midst of those prayers, I know God sees it all, and one day he will redeem all of creation. Until that time, I know our job is "to do justice, and to love kindness, and to walk humbly with your God" (Micah 6:8).

I have learned that the greatest thing in the world is to love. God is love, and he invites us to join him in loving all people regardless of their religion, race, class, or gender. Growing up, I didn't understand this concept, especially in regard to the Khartoum government or Riek Machar, who caused personal suffering for me. I wanted them to suffer as I had suffered. And yet God taught me about the power of love, of hope, and of never giving up.

Even though I am a former refugee from one of the deadliest wars in our history, often I haven't wanted to share my story, because reliving parts of it has been painful. Though many of my friends and work colleagues encouraged me to share, still I battled revealing what I had been through. It would be much easier to focus on helping others heal than exposing my own trauma.

But on March 21, 2014, while I was in the Native American museum in Washington, DC, I came upon an exhibit that challenged my thinking. The exhibit was of a time ball replica. It symbolized a woman's life. The description stated: "A young woman would use a time ball to record her courtship, marriage, and other experiences using a system of knots and beads that only she could decipher. As she grew older, a woman might have several time balls with which to share her life story or keep those memories private. When she passed on, they were buried with her."

I reread that description five times, and each time I reached "When she passed on, they were buried with her," tears streamed down my cheeks. *So if I were to die today*, I thought, *my stories will be buried with me.* How would my children or grandchildren know of me? How would my daughter, Cholie, learn about her heritage and our family background? What stories would I leave behind? How could she know about both happy and sad times of my life when I am no longer here?

Am I going to be buried with my life story? I wondered.

I thought about my relatives. I was still mourning the stories that perished with those who died in the war. I was mourning Dinka knowledge from the grandmas and grandpas, which I could not retrieve. I knew little of my father and mother, since I was orphaned at a young age.

I also thought about the meaning of living authentically. I knew my daughter could handle anything, especially the wounds of my life, because she is a child of God. So for me not to share the truth of my life with her would keep her from the foundation of her heritage. It was at that moment I realized I needed to share my story—not just for Cholie, but for the thousands of orphans who never had the opportunity to share with their families and the world what they had experienced.

And so, this is my story.

Part One

Home

Africa is mystic; it is wild; it is a sweltering inferno; it is a photographer's paradise, a hunter's Valhalla, an escapist's Utopia. It is what you will, and it withstands all interpretations. It is the last vestige of a dead world or the cradle of a shiny new one. To a lot of people, as to myself, it is just home.

—Beryl Markham,
West with the Night

CHAPTER 1

The Joy of Innocence

They're coming closer and closer, and it's harder to fight them off, but we must!" My father pleaded with the village elders. He was a commander in the Sudan People's Liberation Movement/Army (SPLM/A), so everybody listened to his words and respected him. He pulled out a piece of cloth from his pants pocket, revealing the SPLA flag. The colors were black, green, red, blue, and yellow. But what stood out to me was the gold-yellowish star. As my dad held it up, the wind moved the piece of cloth. It fluttered in the breeze, beautiful.

He continued to speak, but at four years old, I wasn't interested in what they were discussing; I was too busy playing. Even if I were interested, I wasn't allowed to listen in. The elders told me to go away because they were having adult talk, and I certainly wasn't an adult.

Because my dad, my *baba*,[1] was a soldier, he was gone from our village most of the time, "fighting against the

---

[1] Dinka contains many loanwords from Arabic, due to the country's past. There are six different dialects of Dinka that have different spellings and grammar. Most Dinka, and especially most former refugees, speak a combination of these dialects, and may include words from Swahili, Arabic, and English in everyday speech. There may also be words in common with Nuer.

oppressors in the Sudanese government to bring freedom to black Africans, *Monyjang*," which was what Dinka people called themselves. But it didn't make much sense to me. Why would Baba and his dress-alike men, whom Baba called soldiers, fight? He was also a Christian, so he said he fought to defend his family and to make sure everyone could have the freedom to live and worship as they wanted.

But I never saw anybody keep anyone in our village from worshiping. Our village had no church, but I always saw the elders say prayers when they sacrificed to the gods. So why fight over that? I had never seen anyone except boys fighting. Sometimes the older people yelled at us kids not to fight or destroy each other's toys, which were made from mud and plants. And that always ended it. Could the adults not do the same?

I overheard stories of the years of *riak* and *pawar* (wars and disasters). These were times when our ancestors struggled because of crop failure, clan wars, and intertribal disputes, but I had never seen anything like that happen. Our village, Aruai Mayen, was quiet, isolated, and peaceful, so isolated and peaceful I didn't even know what "war" meant.

I asked one of my cousins what the war, *tong*, was about. He told me we were enemies with the red people, the Arabs, *Jalaba*, in Khartoum.

I've tried to italicize words that are not found or typically used in the English language—they may have their origin in a wide array of different languages spoken in South Sudan. It's possible that no authoritative source fully captures the vocabulary and grammar used by the South Sudanese diaspora.

"Where is Khartoum?" I asked.

"Very far away."

Adults are crazy, I thought. *Why would anybody fight somebody far away?* Then I thought, *I wish I could travel very far away.* But I couldn't even go into my grandmother's garden, not far from our hut. And if I could travel, I would go with Baba, so I could spend more time with him and help him fight. I thought that would be fun. It must be, since whenever he came home, he always brought me candy and pretty dresses. But then, if I did travel with Baba, I would have to leave my mom and my *kokok*, my grandma, the mother of my father. They would miss me too much.

So Baba was fighting the Jalaba, and that was all I knew. I never met any Jalaba. But I knew they were the enemy.

Whenever Baba came home after being gone a long time, he would shoot off guns to let us know he was arriving, and all the villagers would dress in their best clothing and jewelry and prepare for a special ceremony in which they would kill a cow. At the ceremony the older men and women would sing or make some kind of speech, and then Baba would jump over the dead cow. Kokok told me this was a ceremonial cleansing from the war.

"When a soldier returns to the village after the war, the sacrifice for sin is made to atone them for killing people in the battlefield. When the soldiers fight, they enter a different world that we don't know," she said. "Then they can be reunited with their family and the villagers."

I didn't like it, because Baba would come home but he couldn't greet me and my half siblings until after he'd jumped over the cow. I stood on one side of the cow while he stood on the other. The elder men, whom we called grandpas, sang and chanted until the cow urinated before they killed it. I never saw that happen, though, because I wasn't allowed to go there until the cow was already dead and lying on the ground. As soon as I walked to the place, I looked for my baba. I longed to run to him and throw my arms around him, but Kokok held tightly onto me. She made sure we didn't cheat, because she didn't want Baba to pass the spirit of a dead person from the war to us. Baba said being a Christian, he didn't believe in it, but Kokok did and he wanted to honor her.

After he jumped over the cow, he would pick me up and squeeze me tightly to his chest. My heart flooded with happiness each time. My father was home again and we could all be a happy family once more. Even though I knew he would stay only for a short time, those moments with him gave me joy.

Other soldiers came with him. They all wore camouflage clothing and carried guns. I didn't understand what guns were, since I never saw the soldiers do anything with them except carry them. I just thought they were holding long, odd-looking sticks. I was intrigued, though, since they weren't like the canes the grandpas carried or like the spears the men—whom we called uncles—and boys carried when they tended the cows or went fishing, so one time I drew close to a soldier and touched the gun. It felt like our *sanduk* felt—the cold, rough, metal boxes that we stored cloth, salt, and sugar in.

"Be careful," he told me. "Fire comes out of its mouth." My eyes grew wide and I wanted to know more, but he walked away, leaving me confused and a bit scared.

On his visits home, my father would talk about how the SPLA/rebels' territory was expanding, which cities they were able to capture, and how someday we might win the war and our people would be free. He would say, "We fight because we want our children to have a chance to go to school and to farm freely and without fear."

I didn't understand school because there was no school in our village, but I understood farming. The Monyjang, my Dinka clan, were farmers and raised cattle. The cows were mostly to give us milk or for rituals, marriage dowries, and other cultural occasions. The number of cattle a villager had showed how wealthy he was in the village. Kokok had thousands of cows.

I loved when Kokok would take milk from the cows and turn it into butter; then she would boil the butter for hours to make ghee. The ghee, creamy and a deep golden-orange, was nutty and sweet. When she was finished cooking the ghee, Kokok would call me, my half sister Atong, and the other children to clean the cooking pot. The burned milk solids from the butter were stuck hard to the bottom and we had to scrub it. I didn't mind so much, because I knew how tasty our food was going to be. Kokok used the homemade ghee to cook our food. She could make *anything* taste delicious with it.

Kokok, like the other villagers, had a large garden beyond our hut where she would plant and harvest our food. She never let me go into the garden with her, though, because she told me snakes and scorpions hid in there, and she couldn't keep a good eye on me.

Even if I couldn't go into it, I loved Kokok's garden. It had so many colors and varieties of food. Green vegetables, red and green tomatoes, sorghum, okra, pumpkin, colorful maize, and squash. I loved watching Kokok work in her garden, because she would rustle up the hundreds of butterflies and dragonflies that fluttered through the crops, kissing the leaves. And the birds in the garden! They were covered with colors too. Red, yellow with black heads, blue, turquoise, golden, orange—all so beautiful. Kokok would often shout at the birds to fly away because she didn't want them to eat our crops.

I loved harvest time. When the women would grind fresh corn, sorghum, and other grains, the air around them gave off a lightly sweet smell. Sometimes if we children were especially good, the women would peel the sorghum stems and give them to us to eat. The sweet smells would flood my nostrils as I'd bite off the husk. Then I'd take off the leaves and open the stems. Sometimes the inside was a vivid red—we called these "dove's wine." It was like candy!

I loved looking at all the colors of our village. I saw *alook*, which is a tall, golden grass. It was like a thousand yellow cats turned upside down. The fuzzy tops of the grass always made me feel good. And everywhere I looked around our huts, I saw the greenest greens I'd ever seen. Kokok said our land was the greenest place in the whole world—lush pastures, she called it, made that way because the Nile River's Sudd and her tributaries were so close to our village. We were only a twenty-minute walk to a stream that flowed into the Nile and only a day's walk from the Nile itself. I didn't know much about the Nile, because I had never been there either, but a lot of our village's teens and newlyweds went with the cattle to one of the Nile's larger tributaries and cared for the cows there, especially during the dry season. They called that place Toch. The boys went there and learned how to wrestle and wrote love songs, which they sang to girls they were courting, but then when they came home during the rainy season they sang them for us to learn. The cattle camp sounded exciting to me, and I always begged Kokok and my mother to let me go, but they said I was too young. Kokok promised that when I grew older, I too could go with the others to the Nile to care for the cattle and learn about courtship. Until then I was to stay put and enjoy life in our village.

That was easy to do, because I always found something to keep me busy. I played with other children and explored around our huts. Even though I was the only child of my mother, my father had another wife and children, and they lived near us too. I especially liked to play with Atong, who was one year younger than me. My two older half brothers, Luk and Padiet, didn't want to play. They were too busy doing older boy stuff.

Our village had about a hundred people living in it and was tucked back not far from the main highway, even though I never got to travel on it. It was made up of many mud huts with hard dirt floors—huts we slept in, huts we cooked in, huts for the cows and their babies. The roofs were covered with straw thatch, thick enough to keep the rain out and keep us dry. We didn't have bathrooms, so if we had to relieve ourselves at night, we used a cow's horn, which Kokok set in the wall, like a urinal, or a gourd that we'd empty outside the hut in the morning. If I had to do the other, Kokok or another adult would have to take me outside to Panom, a cleared area away from the huts, where I could relieve myself.

Surrounding our huts were the pastures for all the tribe's cattle, and on the far edge beyond was the forest, though I never went that far. I loved to climb the trees near Kokok's hut or watch the women in our village spend their days collecting food from the garden and cooking, with all the delicious smells. The women talked and laughed as they ground corn and sorghum to make all kinds of food for us to eat. We were never hungry. But we were lean and really tall.

The Dinkas are a tall people—everyone in our village stood like giants, and I knew one day I too would stand tall like the trees of the forest. Kokok said we were the tallest people in all of Africa. My mom was tall, but I noticed that her stomach bulged out bigger than the other women's. She told me that was because she was keeping a baby there, and soon I would get to meet a little brother or sister. That made me happy, because then I would have someone else to play with and care for.

Although I enjoyed playing during the days, it was

always very hot. I liked when the temperature cooled down and the night came to life. In the evenings, the adults set piles of dried cow dung on fire to keep away the tsetse flies and bugs and provide warmth for our cows. Then the adults milked the cows. The cow dung didn't smell too bad. It had a sweet scent to it from all the grass the cattle ate. It was nice out in the open, but I didn't like it when we burned it inside the hut, because the smoke became trapped and made me cough.

At night I especially liked to lie on my mat in Kokok's hut and look through the window at the moon and stars. The sky looked like a deep body of water full of lights. Since our village had no electricity, the moon, stars, the villagers' fires, and fireflies were our only source of light. That was okay with me because they were beautiful as they shone or flickered. I listened to the crickets singing their songs and watched the frogs as they leapt from one place to another and the fireflies as they danced around the leaves.

"Kokok, why is there an ocean above us but water doesn't pour down on us?" I asked her once.

"Because Duchak, the creator, governs the water and tells it when to come and when not to come," she told me. "When it rains, part of the water comes from that deep ocean that snakes itself across the sky at night."

During cloudy nights, I couldn't see this ocean, but when the sky was clear, it was my favorite time. Sometimes I'd see running and dancing stars with burning fire on their tails. It looked like the firewood the elders carried at nighttime. In the stars I could see faces—Baba, Kokok, my family, friends. Night after night when Kokok told us to be quiet and go to sleep, I would lie on my back facing the sky, look up at the stars, and communicate with my family because I could see them there and the stars always smiled back at me.

When the nights were cloudy, I would lie on my mat and listen to the other people lying by me, since our family all slept in the same room. They would often tell stories or play guessing games. I liked listening, even though I didn't understand them because I was too young to know what they were talking about.

I loved my village. I was safe and free to run and play. We had plenty to eat. My family was kind and loved me well. Other than my father being gone a lot, there was nothing else I needed or wanted. I couldn't imagine living any other way.

CHAPTER 2

"They Are Coming!"

The rainy season had come. The cattle sensed it first, lowing and restless. They lined up and pointed their noses in the air in the direction where the rain was coming from. We smelled the rain before we ever saw it. The sky beyond the forest was getting darker. Just as when we'd throw dirt in the air and the dust trailed behind it, we could see sheets of rain below the clouds in the distance.

During this rainy season, Baba was gone from the village again. He was out fighting the enemy I had never seen. Mama's belly had grown to the size of a watermelon, and Kokok said it was getting close for me to have a baby brother or sister. They all wished my father were here to witness the birth, but no one could get word to him.

One day I ran out to play with a friend during a break in the rain. As we laughed and ran, we heard a strange and scary noise.

Tak-tak-tak. Boom! Boom!

It didn't sound like thunder and it didn't sound like when my father came home and shot guns to celebrate. This was louder and more intense. With each sound, my heart jumped a beat and made me feel uneasy.

I ran to Kokok's hut to see if she knew what was happening.

"Don't worry, my child," she told me. "Nothing is going on. They are just testing their weapons in a nearby village, and sometimes they fire them for celebration. Remember when your dad comes home with soldiers and they fire guns? Go back and play. It will be over soon."

The next day, a man showed up at our hut. He was sweaty and acted jumpy. He called my uncle Machok and my grandmother and started whispering.

Tak-tak-tak. Boom! Boom! The blasts had returned and now sounded louder and closer.

I felt my stomach tighten, but reminded myself that Baba was in a neighboring village, so everything was all right. *But why is he not home yet? Why isn't everyone preparing and getting dressed in their best clothes to greet him? Why isn't somebody killing a cow for him to jump over so we can be together and he can hold me?*

Not long after that, my mother began to feel great pains in her stomach, and Kokok swept me out of the hut, telling me it was my mother's time to deliver a baby. The other village women came, as was our custom, and I went to play.

After several hours, with my mother still in labor, I noticed something odd happening in the village. The villagers were grabbing their children and racing toward the pastures. "Quick!" they yelled. "They are coming! Run, run!"

Who is coming? Why do we have to run? I wondered. I didn't believe any of this was really happening. *Maybe the elders are just firing guns to scare us.* I decided the elders were doing as they often did when they told scary stories to keep us from wandering into the forest or grasslands by ourselves.

One of the elders came to our hut and told Kokok, "Our enemies are coming. We must go to the forest."

Enemies? I thought our enemies were in Khartoum. Why would they come here? This was just a simple village with cows and good families. I scooted into our hut, dodging between the women who were now rushing out.

Kokok was moving around the hut, gathering rags and water.

My mother was in the middle of the room on her mat. Her grunts and groans sounded like one of Kokok's cows giving birth. Her face was anguished and sweat dropped from her face like the rain pouring out onto the pastures. How could she run anywhere?

She looked at me and grimaced. "Go, my child," she told me through heavy breaths. "I will be right behind you."

"But . . ." How could I tell her I was afraid? I'd never been to the forest before. What if the lions were there waiting for me?

"You must go," she told me again.

My uncle Machok came to the hut and told me to run. He promised that he and Kokok would stay with my mother and help her get away.

"Rebecca," my mother said and nodded for me to come close to her. Her body smelled of bitter sweat. "I'll be behind you. I love you."

Before I could say anything, my uncle grabbed my arm and hurried me away from my mother.

"Go, go!" he told me.

With hot tears now welling in my eyes and flooding over my cheeks, I went outside and stood, feeling unsure and afraid. Atong stood nearby. She swallowed hard and looked at me.

"We must run, Rebecca!" a woman said, grabbing Atong's and my hands.

We followed the other villagers as they fled. Many of them were already far into the pastures.

Tak–tak–tak. Boom! Boom!

The sounds were closer still.

We headed away from our hut toward the dark cover of the trees, beyond Kokok's garden, beyond the cows in their pasture, farther than I had ever traveled before.

Be brave, I told myself. *Mama is right behind us.* I quickly chanced a look back, but she wasn't there. I slowed down, unsure of what to do.

"Rebecca, hurry up!" the woman holding my hand said.

If our enemy was really coming, my mother and Kokok didn't have much time to catch up with us. Where was my father? Was he fighting against our enemies in the other village? Was he okay?

We reached the edge of the forest and once again I slowed down, thinking we were now safe, but the woman holding on to me urged me deeper into the darkness. The tamarind, palmyra palm, rubber tree—known locally as *quel*—and gum arabic trees were heavy with the wetness of all the rains, and the ground wasn't as soft as the meadow. Sticks and roots jutted out from under the leaf-covered ground, pinching my bare feet. Everywhere I stepped I wondered if I might land on a snake, scorpion, or giant worm or beetle. And the forest felt stiflingly hot, humid, and confining. Onward we raced, past the branches that hit and scratched my face and arms, through the giant spider webs.

How will my mom find me if we go in too far?

Finally, after what felt like hours, and when my legs could keep going no more, we caught up to the rest of the villagers farther and deeper in, where we could no longer see the pastures or our huts. The trees were so thick that even the thin veil of light struggled to show us the way.

Clustered together were the rest of the children in a circle, with the adults surrounding them as protection. The woman holding my hand urged Atong and me forward toward the center.

The bugs swarmed around us, buzzing in our ears and nipping at our skin. I tried swatting them away, but they kept coming back. For hours, we huddled together, listening to the sounds of the deep forest—the rustling leaves, the snail and clam whistles, and the hyenas' harsh cackles. Every movement among the trees brought with it the fear of snakes or lions or other wild animals. I prayed that night not to meet a python, because a boy in our village told me that he saw one eat their goat alive, and I was smaller than a goat. Would a giant python come into our group and hurt us?

In the distance, we could hear the *tat-tat-tat* of the gunfire—now in our village.

The adults said we were being attacked by the Jalaba—the Arabs in the Khartoum government.

"What if they find us?" I asked one of the elders.

"They won't," he told me. "The Arabs are from the north. They do not know the forest as we do."

Nothing made sense to me, and besides, where was my mother? Why was she not here yet? Where were Kokok and my uncle? They were supposed to bring Mama to the forest.

I ignored the growls of my stomach, just wanting to be back home where we had plenty of food and dry clothes and cow dung to light and keep the insects away. I also tried to ignore the sounds of the wild animals in the distance—the howling hyenas and the growling lions.

"Do not fear," an elder told us children. "We will protect you. There are too many of us. They won't bother you. But do not leave this group and go anywhere by yourself."

That was most important when we had to go to the bathroom. One or two adults walked with us away from the group, so we could have privacy. They forbade us to go alone, even just a few feet away, because they didn't want some wild animal to snatch or attack us, so we always went to the bathroom in groups.

By early evening, the gunfire had silenced, but still we waited. Finally, I heard someone coming. The person was wailing. I thought maybe the Beir, or Murle, clan was now attacking people. They were our village enemies too, but I heard they were not red like the Arabs. Women in our village made a special cry when Beir were in the area. They

normally came after our cows. I never saw any of them, but
in my heart I knew they were magical and could hide in
the grass. I couldn't see them but from the stories I heard
from the older children about the Beir people, I knew
they could see me. This cry didn't sound like that, though.
These cries grew closer to us until I spotted a woman walking toward us, holding a bundle of something.

The wails grew louder and fiercer. It was Kokok.

I looked past her to see where my mother was, but only
Kokok joined our group. In her arms was a tiny baby.

"Achol had a baby girl," Kokok told the others through
her sobs.

Usually all the women shouted with joy over a baby's
birth, with everyone taking turns holding the baby, but no
one did. They didn't even chant what they always recited
over every newborn—"*Baai aceng-paandun aceng,*" which means,
"People are living in the land; your home has people in
it, you are protected." They only moaned and shook their
heads.

I didn't understand what they were doing, but I felt
my stomach tighten again, as it had with the sounds of the
blasts.

"Achol is dead. She bled too much. It was just too much
for her to try to run and give birth," Kokok said.

The group of women all began to wail and rock back
and forth.

Kokok's eyes found me and she motioned for me to
come to her. "You have a little sister," she said. Before I
could ask her about my mother, she gently placed the baby

in my arms and showed me how to hold on without hurting her. The baby, snuggled tightly in the wrap, barely moved. I had never seen a newborn baby before. I expected her to look like me, since she was my sister. But her skin was a reddish color.

Is my sister an Arab? The red-skinned people?

"Why is she not dark like we are?" I asked Kokok.

"Because, my child, Dinka babies are lighter when they are born, and their skin becomes darker later to match the soil of our land."

The baby kept her eyes closed peacefully, as though she had no fear or worries. As though she had not been born in a world that had just ripped apart.

"What is her name?" I asked.

"Her name is Akon," Kokok said. I knew what that meant: *ignored, neglected, rejected one.* I swallowed hard. At least for now, Akon was at peace.

I wished I could have felt so innocent and peaceful. I used to feel that way. But no longer.

I had a baby sister, but now no mother. And the war, which had been so distant before, entered our village and destroyed my life.

🐘 🐘 🐘 🐘 🐘

After the attackers were gone and it was safe to return, Kokok left the baby with us and returned to the village to bury my mother.

When we walked back, as I got closer to our hut, I noticed behind it was a patch of fresh dirt, my mother's grave. Our village didn't have a cemetery, so we buried our loved ones behind our huts.

I still didn't understand what death meant. I heard people talking about it, but it made no sense to me. How could my mother be dead? Maybe she was just sleeping. Or perhaps it was a mistake.

"You know, when somebody dies, they might come back," one of my friends said. "Maybe they just put your mom down there for a little bit, so maybe we should dig her out."

That made sense to me. I had to help my mother get free. That would make Kokok stop crying and everyone would be happy again. So my friend and I went to the hut where Kokok kept her gardening tools and we each grabbed a hoe. Back at the fresh dirt, we began to dig.

We dug and dug until we heard my grandmother's voice. "What are you doing?" she said, sounding shrill and looking astonished. Then she began to cry.

Some village women saw what was happening and rushed to Kokok. They told us, "You can't do that."

"But why?" I said. "I'm helping my mother to come out."

Lots of people began to cry then, as they took away the hoes and led us from my mother's grave. "No, she is not coming back," they told me.

I was angry at them. *Why would they do that to her?* I thought. *I was trying to help; now she'll be stuck under the ground.*

But they didn't listen. They just told my friend and me to go play—away from the grave.

What will happen to us all now? I wondered. Everyone's

happiness seemed to be gone. I missed my mom. Instead of playing as the women suggested, I found a quiet spot behind one of the other huts and cried.

The days passed and I tried not to think about my mother's absence. With my father still gone and my mother dead, Kokok took my new sister, Akon, and me as her own children to raise. Although she seemed sad, she tried to cheer me up. She played games with me and showered me with love and food. I ate so well, I grew as wide as I was growing tall.

Most villagers made simple meals of sorghum or grain, but Kokok always cooked meals for me that most people would serve special visitors. She would lay out a meal of sorghum with ghee, along with flatbread, meat, and vegetables. When one of the adults would ask, "Who is your special guest?" Kokok would smile at me and say, "My sweet baby, Rebecca."

"Harrumph," the adult would say.

"Spoiled" was how the villagers described me. The village children were always envious of me. When they saw me, they'd say, "The child of Nyandhotdit is here" (Nyandhotdit was my kokok's name). "Let's beat her up." I think they mostly did it to annoy Kokok or to have an adult run after them. Most adult villagers didn't pay any attention to what the kids did, but Kokok did when it concerned me. There was nothing I wanted or needed that I didn't receive.

One day about a month after the attack, the villagers started shouting and running again. The attackers had returned and we had to flee. Kokok grabbed my hand, picked up the baby, and we headed back toward the dark, scary forest.

We didn't have anything to eat or drink to keep our energy up. Everything happened so quickly, no one had a chance to bring anything, and I grew cranky.

"I'm thirsty," I told Kokok.

"I know, sweet child. I am too, but we don't have anything. Try not to think about it."

But the more I tried not to think about being thirsty, the more thirsty I became. My throat was parched and my stomach growled nonstop. Akon even started to cry, her wails mixing with the raindrops that were now coming down. Kokok tried to quiet her, but she had nothing for her to drink.

The next day we continued to hide, fearful that the soldiers, who now knew the general direction of our escape, were waiting to ambush us. So we stayed put, hoping and praying they were gone. Hoping and praying our village was still intact. But knowing nothing for sure.

Another day passed with no food or water. Akon continued to cry, but eventually her cries grew weaker and weaker as she became more dehydrated and didn't have cow's milk to drink. Kokok tried to gather up some of the water from the rains, but it wasn't enough to quench any of our thirst.

I was tired, achy, scared, and cold, but thrilled when we finally received the okay to leave the forest and return to our huts.

Our village looked the same as when we'd run away.

The cows were still grazing in the pastures, the garden was still overflowing with vegetables.

I raced to our water supply and filled my stomach with as much water as it could hold! I just wanted something to drink and to get back to playing.

Even though we hadn't seen the soldiers and even though everything in the village appeared to be the same, it wasn't. The evil men had stolen from me again. Within twenty-four hours of returning to the village, my baby sister was dead.

CHAPTER 3

What No Child Should See

Life became peaceful again for a while, long enough that
I no longer thought about the war or our escapes into the
scary forest. Every few months Baba continued to come
and go from our village. One day I caught him crying. I
asked Kokok why my big strong baba was crying like a child.
Kokok said that whenever Baba saw one of the women from
the village wearing my mama's clothes, he cried. Kokok
told me that I used to cry too, so they collected all the
clothes and put them away until I would forget. That surprised me, because I didn't remember it. I tried to think
of that, but it had been too long a time. I couldn't even
remember what my mama looked like. One day when Baba
was home, Kokok told me she didn't know how long he
would be around, because the army has reassigned him to
a different area to fight called Ethiopia, or what we called
Abyssinia. When he left, I didn't see him again for more
than a year. I was six years old now.

I barely remembered my mother's face, although I
could still remember her voice, and sometimes I wished
she were there with me.

With all her six children grown, I became Kokok's

child. She was always affectionate toward me, calling me her baby, *nyanpieth,* her pretty girl. Although I still loved to play with Atong and my other friends, I preferred to stay near Kokok. She was so very tall, like the akot—palmyra palm trees—of our forest, and carried a long spear everywhere she went. She made me feel safe. My grandmother was as well armed as the men of our village. She was the only woman who carried the weapons the men carried. She was also one of the elders of our village. I loved that she was my kokok, because that made me feel important too.

She wore a leather skirt decorated with shells down the sides. In the front she'd sewn coins, some silver and some gold. On the face of the coins were images of men and women I had never seen before. Her ears were pierced all the way around and each hole held a shiny silver hoop. The hoops started small at the top of her ears and they became bigger and bigger as they moved down to her lobe. And she wore lots of jewelry around her neck and arms. No one else in the village wore such beautiful things. But the best part of the way she dressed was how she sounded. With each step, her clothes and jewelry clanked together, making the most lovely rhythms. I loved to follow her around, just to hear her skirt sing. Even though our village didn't have a radio or television, my grandmother was my music.

The only place I went without Kokok was to a new church. She didn't go because she didn't approve of it. One of the neighbors' kids took me to the other side of the village where the church was. I loved going every Sunday. We sang, danced, and learned stories about Jesus. I was falling in love with Jesus and I loved Kokok, and I wanted them to meet! Every Sunday I came home and told Kokok she needed to go to church with me. "You have to be a Christian," I told her. "It's really fun and there's this person called Jesus." I told Kokok how I wanted to be like him. I didn't understand much of what they said about him, but I did want to travel far from my village and meet people from other villages, just like he traveled.

"Mm-hmm," she always said. "I've heard about him."

One particular Sunday in the fall, I returned home and was telling Kokok about Jesus again, when at about noon I noticed the skies getting dark as night. The rains were coming. I never minded the rains so much; it was the thunder and lightning that terrified me. The thunder was so loud it would shake the earth and our huts, and the lightning cracked, making me jump. I stayed close to Kokok because she wasn't afraid. I knew she would always protect me.

The rain fell hard and heavy all day and night. When I finally went to sleep, I drifted off to the sounds of the rain pelting our thatched roof and the thunder clapping painfully close.

I dreamed that I saw the rains flooding the floor of our hut. Deeper and deeper the water became as I stood on my mat surrounded by what had become a lake. The raindrops were giant and made large splashing sounds. The drops were falling hard as usual, but as they hit the ground, they turned to fire. And as they hit the pond of water surrounding me, the water turned red and smoke floated up from it. The more the raindrops joined the burning water, the bigger the fire became, until it created a huge blast, suffocating me in the middle of it.

I awoke crying and screaming.

Kokok was at my mat immediately. "What's wrong, baby?" she said as she knelt beside me.

Though the rain was still falling outside, all was dry in the hut.

"A fire! The water turned to fire and I was in the middle of it and—"

"Oh, child, it's just a dream," she said, her voice soothing me.

"But—"

"No need to worry." She wrapped her arms around me and rocked me. "Kokok is here. There's nothing to be afraid of. You're safe with me. I won't let anything happen to you."

The warm hands of Kokok, along with the dim lightning from far off and the animals' whistles, mixed together with the soft raindrops, and put me back to sleep. All was secure.

Three days later another attack came.

🐾 🐾 🐾 🐾 🐾

The sun had just set when the sound of a distant cannon blast echoed into our village.

Boom!

All night, the same sound: *boom!*

Kokok didn't look concerned, so I knew I shouldn't be

either, but I had to know if we were in danger, since the last time I heard those noises an attack came.

"Nothing to be worried about, my child," Kokok promised me when I asked her about it.

But in the morning, the danger drew nearer.

I was just outside Kokok's hut when Uncle Dau Ajang stopped by our house to talk with Kokok. I overheard him say something about Deng Awel testing guns in Padiet, a nearby village. I was confused to hear the name Deng Awel, because that was my dad's name.

Is Baba back? I thought, excitement growing within me. *He will have a dress for me! But why is he in Duk Padiet? Why does he not come straight here?*

Something wasn't right. As Atong and I played, people started stopping by the hut more frequently and whispering to my grandmother. I couldn't make sense of what they were saying, but I knew it wasn't good. They all carried the same look in their eyes as when a lion has eaten one of their cows or when a boy has gotten lost in the rain while looking for straying cattle. But why were they whispering? They had never done that before.

When a man I didn't know came, I snuck close to Kokok so I could overhear them talking. "There has been an attack," the man said. "The soldiers are coming, and they aren't only the Arabs. Riek Machar, one of the SPLA generals, has defected and joined the northern government. He's from Nuer. He and the other Nuer have been sent by a devil called Wurnyang and the Khartoum government to fight the Dinka people."

My ears perked up. I knew about Nuer—they were not far from us and they were our village friends. They normally came during the dry season to take their cattle to the cattle camp, just as we did. Kokok always gave them food and anything they needed for their journey. Kokok and most people from my village also spoke their language. But they always came during the dry seasons, never during the rainy season.

I heard the man tell Kokok that the Arabs were using local people who knew about the hiding places in the forest. They were sure to find and attack us. Then the man told Kokok we needed to flee and take everything with us, because they knew where we would hide and would come into the forest after us. "They're calling this the Bor Massacre. You must go quickly," he said. "They are planning a big attack—on this village too. They want to destroy everything *and* everyone. You don't have much time!"

At that time most men and youth of our village had left for Nhial, or what we called heaven or a faraway land, or to Abyssinia. I knew this because my half brothers and my friend's brothers went to Ethiopia to go to school and to become soldiers. They were known as the Jiech el Amer—the Red Army. They were seeds of the black SPLA, the seed of John Garang, the founding father of South Sudan. They were to replace my baba's generation and continue fighting the war when the others got too old. When I heard about them, I figured they were just fighting play wars like the boys in our village did.

Some of the elders said it was better for the few men

and boys to be gone so our enemies couldn't come to the village and force them to fight on their side.

Uncle Machok was listening too, and he told Kokok he would alert everyone. Uncle Machok hadn't left the village with the other men, because we needed a male from our family to protect us, since all his brothers, including my dad, were gone.

I watched as the man ran from our village to alert a neighboring village with the same news. I stood, unsure what to do, as my grandmother gathered maize, cooking oil, sorghum, and a cooking pot. I heard the sounds of the *achuil*, the African fish eagle, and I looked into the sky and saw a few of them swarming over us, as though they sensed the danger and wanted to prey upon us and steal our food. I ran to Kokok's grain storage area to warn the hen and her chicks that trouble was coming for them too. To my surprise the hen was already under the storage hut and had already covered her chicks beneath her. I was happy she was protecting her family.

When I ran back to Kokok's hut, I saw her look around, as if she were trying to decide if we had time to take anything else. Then she looked at me. For the first time in my life, I saw fear in my strong, proud grandmother's eyes.

"Come, child. We must hurry," she told me, as she stepped out of our hut and toward the forest once again. Carrying only the clothes I wore, I raced to keep up with her long strides. As I looked at my tall kokok, I saw white egrets flying over the herd of cows ahead of her. My neck hurt looking up, so I looked down and saw butterflies, dragonflies, and other small insects and frogs jumping over the grass. They didn't know trouble was coming.

As we hurried past the cow hut, I saw people throw rope leashes over their cattle's necks and lead them across the pasture and into the forest. Normally our cows grazed without ropes on their necks, but that day they all had to drag the ropes around. I overheard someone say we were going to lead the cattle to the Nile, where they went during the dry season.

My heart leapt. I had always wanted to go there, but Kokok had never let me, saying I was too young. Now I would get to see it for myself!

If we made it.

This time we weren't as quick as the attackers. They were already in the village, setting huts on fire and shooting toward us. The familiar *tak-tak-tak, boom, boom* was the closest I'd ever heard before.

Because of the rainy season, the pastures were filled and soggy, slowing us down. My legs couldn't keep up with everyone else. And the blinding, spitting rain now coming down made it difficult to see where I was going.

Tss tss tss. A hissing sound whizzed past my ear, and then another and another. The sounds mixed with the shouts and screams of the villagers.

"Bullets! Run faster!" somebody yelled.

I felt something speed by my arm and send chills all over my body. I tried speeding up but the rain and the mud felt too thick to push through. I felt as if I were going in slow motion. As I finally entered the edge of the forest,

I tripped over a root and fell. I felt a strong sting land on the side of my leg and the worst pain I'd ever experienced shot out from it. I looked down at my leg, but my dark skin against the dark forest showed me nothing.

"Come on, Rebecca. Run!" Kokok told me, but I couldn't move. I sobbed and limped behind Kokok, now terrified the attackers were getting closer. I could hardly breathe. This had been my dream: the fire and explosions all around me. And what was worse—I'd been shot.

🌸 🌸 🌸 🌸 🌸

The pain was terrible, but I couldn't stop or the bullets would catch me. All I could do was limp.

We zigzagged and darted through the trees, working to make sure the soldiers couldn't follow or find us. Onward, deeper into the forest once again we headed, and all my fears returned. The pain made my already-tired legs ache, and I wondered for the first time if I might die and be buried next to my mother.

As soon as we made it to the group's hiding spot, Kokok knelt down to feel my leg. As her large hands rubbed over the area, she breathed a sigh of relief. "You haven't been shot," she said. "You must have hit something sharp when you fell or you got stung." She sighed again.

She might have felt relieved, but I didn't. Shot or no, my leg hurt!

My uncle told me to rub my leg hard to get the cramp out of it.

We walked through the dense forest, past the place

we had hidden the other times, deeper and deeper. I had never been this far before and stuck close to Kokok, afraid that behind every tree or bush crouched a lion or hyena in wait.

We stayed put that whole day and into the night. No one spoke or even whispered for fear the attackers would discover us. Every movement or crack of a branch made us tense up in terror. Even though the temperature was hot, the constant rains falling and the darkness of the forest made us shiver. We couldn't light a fire for warmth, in case the smoke gave us away.

That night the rains continued, and although the weather was usually hot and muggy, lying out in the rain with no blanket, no shoes, and only a thin dress, I couldn't keep myself warm.

The rain beat down on us all night, with the tree overhang giving us little protection. All the children lay in a huddle with the adults lying around us in a circle. Soon the water rose up around us until it came up to my neck and shoulders. Lying in a puddle of cold water, my teeth chattered, my leg ached, and all I could think of was what snake or leech or biting snail or giant beetle might float by me and have me as a meal.

By the next morning, we were still afraid to return to our village, so we kept walking. After what seemed like hours, the forest began to grow thinner and I could see a small clearing ahead with a few huts. Kokok told me we were two villages away from ours. It was vacant—they must have gotten the news and run away too—so the elders decided to stop there for the night. It was time to milk the cows, so my uncle, Kokok, and the others milked the cows they were able to bring with them, and then we ate and got some sleep.

The next morning Mama Yar went to milk the cows again and I followed her. She was married to one of my uncles who had gone to Ethiopia with my baba, leaving her with us. Some of our villagers had started a cow dung fire that morning to keep the flies off the cows. The smoke made things seem foggy. As Mama Yar was milking a cow, suddenly the booming and shooting sounds started. Men with guns and spears came running through the forest toward us. They ran past the cattle, scaring them. Cows were mooing their loud protests and people were screaming and running everywhere. Bullets were whizzing around us. Some of the soldiers were teenagers. They carried long sticks and began beating us over the head. We had no time to run away.

The soldiers yelled at us to sit down, as they hit us and threatened to kill us. I sat next to Kokok. Uncle Machok and several of the other villagers had gotten away and were hiding somewhere in the forest. I stared at these men and boys surrounding us and felt confused. All this time everyone told me we were fighting a war against the red-skinned Arabs. But these boys were black like us.

They threatened us for a while longer, and then they grabbed all the ropes and stole our cattle. Every last one. They spared our lives, but without our cattle, how would we survive?

When the men left, my uncle and the other men returned and told us we could go back to our village. Kokok picked up her cooking pot, and I helped carry some of the food, and we slowly made our way home.

We walked through grass that was thick and tall, and it scared me. I was praying that we would not run into lions or snakes. When the lion roared at night, I was terrified— it was as if it was coming to eat me. Snakes were just as sneaky. I heard their venom was poisonous and deadly. I remembered following a giant snake one time. I had never seen such a large creature. Kokok told me it was a python and I should stay far away, because they ate calves and goats and even children.

After several hours we passed through the village closest to ours where some of our Dinka tribe lived. No one was in sight, which was odd because fires were lit and heating the cooking pots. There was a terrible mess all over and a crazy smell like a dead snake.

Some of the children and I snuck a peek into the cooking pots. Squash and sorghum were cooking inside, which made my stomach growl to life. It had been hours since our last meal and I was hungry! I couldn't understand why no one was watching over the pots. Where was everyone? I asked Kokok if I could have some of the food, but she shook her head. Her face looked sad.

Mama Yar told me to move away from the scattered dishes and to walk quickly away from the village. But she wasn't walking away. The adults were all looking in the huts. Why did I have to leave them?

To take my mind off my hungry stomach, I decided to walk along the edge of the village where there was a tobacco field. The plants were high and I could get lost in them, so I knew not to wander too far. But as I walked along the edge of the field, I saw somebody's legs sticking out from the plants. Kokok always told me that when the tobacco plants flowered, we had to remove the flower because it had something to do with making the plant too bitter. But sometimes the plant smell would make her dizzy, and she would lie down and ask me to get her some water.

I walked slowly toward the person's legs and saw he was wearing light blue shorts, the color of the sky. He must have gotten too dizzy from the plant smell.

"Hey, Grandpa," I said, since we called all our elders either Aunt, Uncle, Grandpa, or Grandma. "Grandpa, get up. They have taken our cows, and people are running now."

He didn't reply.

I couldn't see the rest of his body since he was lying too far among the plants. I leaned down and shook his leg. "Grandpa, are you dizzy? Do you want me to get you water? People are running. You need to get up." I started pulling his leg to awaken him. "Grandpa, you can't sleep here. We must go."

Mama Yar rushed over to me. "Oh, this baby with her quick feet and eyes!" she said. "What am I going to do with you? What is wrong with you? Didn't I tell you not to look around but only where your feet go? Why did you go looking for things you are not supposed to see?"

"Mama Yar," I told her. "This man is dizzy. This happens sometimes to Kokok when she rests in the garden. I am trying to tell him to run with us."

"He is dead," she said. "He was killed last night."

"What?" I didn't understand what she was telling me. No, he was just dizzy from working in the field. Didn't she know that?

"That person is dead," she repeated. "This whole family got attacked. Look at the mess all around here. Can you see how things are?" I looked back toward the huts. The scattered dishes, the cooking pots, the empty huts—it all made sense. I looked again at the man and squinted into the row of tobacco plants. The upper part of his body was covered in blood.

My heart slammed against my chest and I couldn't breathe.

I had never seen a dead body before. When my mother died, Kokok buried her while we were still hiding in the forest. And when my sister died, she just looked like she was asleep. And when the old people in our village died, I never saw them because children were not allowed to go to the burial place. But this man—he died a violent death with blood everywhere.

I had to get away—as far from this man and this place as I could. This was what everyone was talking about? This was war? When men with guns and boys with sticks and spears charged into your village and your home and beat you and stole your cattle and took everything from you, including your life?

Why was no one running?

I raced to Kokok, who was standing near the cooking pots and talking to some of the other women. I pulled on her arm. "Kokok, please! Please, we must run away from here!" I was only six, but I knew I never wanted to see that sight again. I knew something was dark and evil about this place. And I knew I wouldn't forget the sight of that blood. Ever.

CHAPTER 4

"You Must Go"

Smoke hung over our village. As we broke from the forest
and stepped into our pasture, the smell of smoldering ash
filled my nostrils. From a distance, I could see my beautiful village, my home, was no more.

Most of the huts had been burned to the ground. Those
still standing had bullet holes in the walls or their thatched
roofs were burned. Kokok's remained, but the inside was
ransacked. Our things thrown around or smashed.

The calabash used for water was broken. The gourd for
storing milk was in pieces. Stored food and Kokok's seeds
of different plants were scattered around.

All our cattle were gone. The chickens were all stolen.
The garden was stripped bare.

Why? I thought, hot, salty tears threatening to spill
down my face. *Why would somebody do this to us?* We'd done
nothing wrong. We were just living our lives, playing,
laughing, sleeping, eating, resting. We bothered nobody.
Kokok often fed strangers who passed through our village. I couldn't understand why anybody who didn't know
us would want to hurt us and our livestock, want to change
our way of life. I couldn't understand hate.

I didn't even know these men, yet they had stripped everything from me. For what purpose?

"Kokok?" I looked to my grandmother for answers, but she had none to give.

She gazed over what was left of our village. Her tight, pursed lips and sad eyes showed me she must have been thinking the same as me.

"Why do they want to hurt us?" I finally whispered.

Kokok sighed and shook her head. "I don't know, my child. Some men are evil and they want what others have. We have this beautiful land, and they want it."

I wandered around the village, looking at all the destruction—but everywhere was the same. Burned roofs, bullet holes, debris scattered. It reminded me of the village we'd just left, where I saw the dead man. I wanted to run far away—but where could I go where I would be safe? If home was no longer safe, then no place was. There was no laughing today, only moaning.

My father had gone away from our village to fight the enemy. But when the enemy came to us, he was not here to protect us. I wondered why he hadn't come to fight them here where we needed him.

That evening when the cattle normally came in from the pasture to be milked and settled for the night, no cattle came. My uncle would always start a fire made from the cow dung to keep the flies away, but he made no fire this night.

"There will be no milk tonight," Kokok said. "But I will make sorghum." She went to her special storage place

41

that the soldiers hadn't destroyed and pulled out dried meat. She made us a stew out of it.

As I lay on my mat, I looked up at the stars that had so often brought me peace and comfort. At least they hadn't changed. I imagined my mother and sister up there, looking down on me.

For two days we helped the villagers clean up and try to get our lives back to normal. Although we no longer had cattle, Kokok was determined to do what she could to preserve what was left of our life in the village. She spent time in the garden, cleaning it up, and in the evenings she cooked us stews with sorghum. I missed the fresh milk and cheese I was used to.

Four days later the soldiers returned again. This time we had no warning.

🐄 🐄 🐄 🐄 🐄

"Where are your men?" The soldier stood in the doorway of our hut. A rifle rested against his chest, reminding us that he was no friend.

If Kokok was afraid, she didn't show it. "I don't know," she said simply.

I'd never heard my grandmother lie before. Those men who were still in our village, who hadn't gone to fight, were fishing in one of the Nile's tributaries. They would be home before dark.

The soldier must have known Kokok wasn't telling the truth because he walked into our hut and pointed at my uncle's mat, where some of his clothes were. "What are those?"

Kokok only shrugged.

The soldier grabbed the clothes and turned back to Kokok. "Where is your food? Your sugar and salt?" Before Kokok could answer, the man spotted a box next to her that held our sugar. He pushed her out of the way and took the box.

When he left, Kokok and I hurried to the doorway. Soldiers had done the same to the other villagers—taking their clothes and food supplies as well.

"Why did those men take clothes?" I asked Kokok.

"They need them for themselves. They are far from home, so they need our men's clothing. But it is never good to take these things the way they took them. They are stealing from us."

When night fell, my uncle and the other men returned with fish. I thought the fresh cow dung smelled bad, but the fish smelled worse! I struggled eating, because the meat was all bones. Kokok removed the bones before she gave it to us, but she didn't get them all. We ate a good meal, but it wasn't the same without having milk and cheese.

I asked Kokok if we were *abuor* now. That was the name I heard other kids use to tease the children in our village who were poor, whose families didn't have cows. Every time these kids joined the other village kids to play, the mean kids would say, "Abuor smells so bad, like fish." They'd also sing a song that said when abuor saw cows, they'd set the grass on fire so the cows couldn't eat and would die. I had a sense that abuor was not good, but I didn't know why. I didn't mind how the fish tasted; I just didn't want to smell like one or have any of the children make fun of me.

Kokok said, "Keep quiet, child. Don't ever call abuor upon us. Our cows will come back in no time." Then she opened a different metal box the soldier hadn't seen, pulled out a good-smelling soap, and started washing my hands.

Kokok and my uncle talked about the soldiers. They both agreed the soldiers would return.

The next morning my uncle rose early and disappeared into the forest. They knew if he remained, the soldiers would gun him down. At least they weren't killing the women, elders, and children yet, Kokok told him. Then Kokok gathered up what little food and clothing we had left and hurried me to the other side of the village, to Grandpa's house, one of the elders. Other women and children were already there when we arrived. Kokok said our chances for survival were greater if we all stayed together. His hut also had a levee encircling it, so we all had a large, dry patch of land to sit on, since we wouldn't all fit in his hut. Most huts were flooded because it was rainy season and there were no men to build levees out of mud to keep the water away.

Atong was there so I grabbed her hand. We could comfort each other. Atong's baby sister, Nyanguom, my other half sister, sat next to Mama Yar. I loved Nyanguom, because I helped take care of her. We didn't have dolls, so Nyanguom was my baby doll.

Kokok squatted in front of us. "This is very important. When the soldiers come back, they might ask where your baba or his family are, and they'll say his name. They might ask because your baba is in the army. You must say you don't know. That they all went to Ethiopia. They are not even in the village. Do you understand?"

I nodded, even though I didn't really.

The next day soldiers returned to our village. Just as Kokok predicted, they asked, "Do you know the Deng Awel family? Where are they?"

The women said, "We don't know. They went to Ethiopia."

"No, you know them, and you know where they are." They looked at Mama Awal. Unlike most women in our village, she had a decorative marking inked on her forehead. She was a close friend of Kokok's and often came to our hut to visit.

A soldier grabbed Mama Awal and dragged her to the other side of the levee, to a large flooded area just outside the hut.

"Where is everything?" the soldier demanded.

"I don't know, I don't know!" Mama Awal said.

"You are Bor! Look at the mark on your forehead! You have city things. Show us!" He shoved her face into the water and held her tightly as she struggled. All the women started screaming for the soldier to stop, but the boys with long spears and guns pointed them at us and spoke in another language.

"What are they saying?" one of the women asked Kokok.

"To keep quiet or we'll be next," Kokok said.

I was surprised Kokok understood their language. Some of the others in our village did too, because they started talking to the boys in their language. I didn't understand what they were saying, but it looked like they were trying to save Mama Awal.

The boys turned back to Mama Awal and the one soldier shoved her head in the water again and again until she started crying.

I started crying too. I had never heard or seen an older person cry before. Only children cried in the village. But her crying sounded scary, like a cow who was being attacked by a lion. The sounds made my chest and stomach hurt.

Finally the boys left Mama Awal and moved on, looking on their own for the supplies they wanted. The women quickly pulled her out of the water. She gasped and choked and threw up. The women slowly moved her into the hut where she lay for a long time. I was afraid to get close to her, so I stood near the doorway and looked in. She opened her eyes and saw me.

"Rebecca, get me some water. I'm thirsty," she told me. Her voice sounded weak and raspy. I wanted to obey her, since she was my elder, but I was afraid to. I didn't know what to think of the water. She wanted to drink something that had almost killed her. And the way she had been crying when they put her head under the water made me afraid if I gave her water, she would cry again.

Mama Yar told me to get the water, but when I didn't move, she got some and gave it to Mama Awal. I followed Mama Yar, hiding behind her, as I stared at Mama Awal's eyes. They were very red.

She drank the water and then looked at me. Then she

grabbed my hand. "How are you doing, nyanpieth?" When she called me *nyanpieth*, which means "beautiful" in Dinka, my fear went away, because I knew I was talking to Mama Awal. Her voice was familiar—it no longer sounded like the noises she made when the soldiers were soaking her head in the water. She cleared her throat as her voice was cracking in midsentence, like a person with a terrible cold.

Suddenly the soldiers were yelling and running back toward us, beating the women with their fists and the ends of their rifles. Mama Yar had started breastfeeding my cousin Nyanguor. She couldn't run while breastfeeding, so Kokok rushed to take the baby. Just in time. One boy grabbed Mama Yar and started beating her hard on the face and head.

Then he turned from Mama Yar and grabbed the baby out of Kokok's arms. "I know how to make her talk," he said. He carried Nyanguor to the place where Mama Awal had almost drowned and squatted down. He looked at Mama Yar again and lowered the baby into the water.

"No!" Mama Yar yelled. "I will show you where everything is."

Mama Yar took the men to Kokok's garden and pointed to a raised area covered with mud. The men dug until they pulled out five boxes of clothing. One of the boxes was full of colorful seedbeads. I'd never seen these beads before. They were beautiful.

The men grabbed at the strings and some of the beads fell to the ground. As the men moved on to the next boxes, I snuck over and played with the beads in the dirt.

They opened another box and pulled out my favorite flowered dress that I loved to wear to church. With every item they yanked out of the boxes, it felt like a slap against my skin. They divided our clothes among themselves like hungry lions ripping the skin off defenseless sheep.

"I'm going to stop them," I told Mama Yar, feeling angered that they could do such things to us.

"No, Rebecca. Let them be. Otherwise, they will kill us. Remember what they did to Mama Awal."

After they sorted through our clothes, they demanded to see the food. "Where is the sugar? Where is the soap?"

Mama Yar walked slowly as if her feet were chained, and with shaking hands, she pointed to another spot in the garden.

After they had taken everything, they left. Now we really had no food, no clothing, nothing to protect us or keep us alive.

When my uncle returned that night, Kokok told him, "I have never seen this kind of war before, and this is not good. You need to go. Take the children and get far away from here. Head toward Toch or the Bor area, because there you will be close to the SPLA. Maybe you will run into your brother Deng. Tell him he needs to come home and protect his village and not fight the faraway war."

As soon as she said *Toch*, my ears perked up. I knew of that place! That was where the villagers took our cows during dry season. *We are going to the Nile!* I thought, now feeling happy to hear the news. I had always wanted to go there, but Kokok had always said I wasn't old enough.

"But what about you?" my uncle said.

She shook her head. "I will stay here, but I want you to take them. Keep them safe."

She was sending me away and not coming too? My mind couldn't believe what I was hearing. When my dad was leaving for Ethiopia and he was going to take my sisters and me, Kokok refused, saying, "You will not take my babies to some land where they don't teach people values and morals, where they don't respect life." But now she was sending us away—and she wasn't even coming?

I ran forward and grabbed Kokok's hand. "You need to come with us! I need you to come with us."

She looked down at me and smiled, but her eyes looked dark, afraid. "I must stay behind to care for the garden," she told me. She promised to grow crops so we would have something to eat when we returned.

My uncle and Kokok decided that Uncle, his wife—Mama Adau, who was pregnant—Mama Yar, Atong, Nyanguom, Nyanguor, and I would leave in the morning. I didn't want to leave Kokok, but I knew we would be back home soon and I was excited to go on this adventure.

The next morning, Kokok woke me early. I had nothing to take with me, since the soldiers had taken all our clothes and shoes. I just had the dress I'd worn the day before, along with some sandals on my feet.

About an hour before we left, Kokok called me to her. She still had her favorite water bowl, and she began to wash my feet as if they would not get dirty the second I put them back on the ground. Water and mud were everywhere. The

Nile had flooded because it was rainy season. She bent over the levee and collected water from the flooded side and poured it on my legs and feet. As she washed them, she muttered words I couldn't make out. Every now and then, though, I'd hear her say, "Can't take bones of old people to unknown lands" and "My children, go in peace."

I thought it was odd that she was doing this ritual, since I'd never seen her do it before for any of the boys or girls who went to the cattle camp. But I accepted that Kokok was wishing us well for our journey.

"Rebecca," she finally said when she was finished. "When your uncle says, 'Walk,' you need to walk, because now you don't have your dad's bodyguards to help you or people from the village to carry you all the time. You must walk on your own." She hugged me tightly. "I wish the soldiers hadn't taken my seedbeads. I would have made you *goor*, so you could wear it on this journey."

My eyes grew big. A goor was a special Dinka corset that all the beautiful aunts and uncles who went to Toch wore. Goor also told the generations or the status of a family. It protected girls from boys, Kokok once told me. But why did she want me to wear one when I was just six years old and only going to be gone for a few days?

"I know you are too young to wear it," she continued. "But I'd love to see you in it on this journey." She smiled sadly at me. "Be strong and enjoy the cattle camp. Remember, you always ask me about going to Toch, and now is your time to go."

"Okay, Kokok."

She hugged me again. "One more thing, my baby. When men like the ones who came yesterday ever come to you and start beating people, don't cry. Be a strong baby. Don't cry! When you cry, they will take you with them. Do you want that?"

I thought back to the water and how the men had hurt Mama Awal. "Oh, no. No, Kokok," I said. "I will not cry."

She looked at my uncle, Mama Adau, and Mama Yar. "You are taking my child. I don't want to hear that anything has happened to her. I want you to take good care of her. I will meet you again. Now you must go."

Everyone started walking down the gray mud road away from our village. I hesitated. I wanted to hug Kokok one more time.

"You go now, baby." She looked at me without her usual jubilant smile. "I will see you when you come back. I want to hear all about the cattle camp."

"Okay, Kokok."

"I will see you soon," she said.

"See you soon, Kokok!" My voice blended with the hot wind. I raced to catch up with my family. When I turned my head to look back, Kokok was on her knees with her head against the ground. I thought maybe she was picking something up. After a moment I turned around again to see her—I wanted her to look at me and wave good-bye. But when I looked again, her head was still down.

I smiled, thinking of her final words to me. "I will see you soon," she'd said.

And I believed her.

Part Two

Gone

When the people who survived the crossing finally reached us, they said that more than two thousand people had been shot, drowned, or eaten by crocodiles. It was one of the darkest days for southern Sudanese black souls.

—Benson Deng, *They Poured Fire on Us from the Sky*

CHAPTER 5

The Long Road

We must go through the forest and make our own *kuer*," Uncle Machok said. "That is the only safe way."

We were going to make our own road? "How do we make a road, Uncle?" I asked. "The roads are so long. Will the enemy catch us if we start making one?"

"No, child, we will make a road by walking!"

I was confused. Why would we need to make a road when the roads we traveled on had always been there? We headed into the forest and constantly zigzagged. Sometimes we walked through the forest and sometimes where the land was cleared, but never over dirt roads. Whenever we got close to a road, Uncle Machok would look at the mud on it and say, "No, we can't take this road." He'd point out the footprints. "See those bootprints? Soldiers are close by. It's not safe. Let's go back." Once we saw a lot of dead cows on the road. Uncle said they'd been shot.

We passed the village where I'd seen the dead man in the field. I wanted to get past that place quickly.

Walking through the forest was difficult, because so many roots got in our way, and it was dark under the tree canopy. The forest floor was wet with standing water from all the rains. My clean feet and sandals, which Kokok had so carefully washed before we left home, were caked with mud, and I could feel blisters forming. I kept stubbing my toes on the tree roots. It was difficult to keep my eyes on the ground to watch for the roots when I kept having to swat away at the mosquitoes buzzing all around us. I felt as if my skin were covered with them.

When we'd get to a clearing in the forest, I'd see that my arms and legs were covered with bite marks. The mosquitoes were just as bad in the clearings and I'd keep hitting at them, but they just kept coming back. The clear areas weren't easier to walk through, because the grass was tall and it got tangled. Uncle Machok led the way and forced the grass down. He chopped at it and walked back and forth through it, and then he told us, "Okay, now you can come through." Even then, though, I struggled to walk over it.

I'd never walked so far in my life. My legs ached. The air was thick and muggy and my dress stuck to my body. The longer we hiked the more tired I became, and I often tripped and fell. I wished my uncle, Mama Adau, or Mama Yar would carry me, but Mama Adau was pregnant, and they were all carrying our few belongings, my newborn cousin, Nyanguor, and my younger half sister, Nyanguom. Atong and I had to walk on our own.

I wish Kokok were here, I thought. *She would carry me.* Instead of making me feel better, though, thinking of Kokok made me feel even worse. I didn't want to walk anymore; I wanted to go back home and play, eat, sleep in my own bed, and watch all the beautiful butterflies in Kokok's garden.

But then I remembered the soldiers had destroyed her garden and taken all our food.

"When will we be there?" I whined. Uncle told me we would be there soon, but soon never seemed to come. And then after a while, when I'd ask, everyone ignored me. "Why is it taking so long? I'm thirsty! Can't we stop and sit for a while?" But they met these questions too with silence. Atong and I both started whining louder the farther we traveled, until finally my uncle sighed and turned to me.

"Rebecca, we must keep going. The soldiers are killing people here, so we have to go."

My eyes grew big at his words, as the thought came to my mind of the dead man lying in the field with his blue shorts. I swallowed hard and nodded.

I tried to keep walking and not complain, remembering my promise to Kokok that I would be good and listen to my uncle, but even after Uncle's warning, I couldn't help myself. I was tired!

As we continued to walk, I started to hear a loud noise I'd never heard before. It sounded like something crashing into the land.

"What is that?" I asked Uncle.

"That is water," he said simply.

I didn't understand. How could water sound like that? It wasn't so loud back home.

"There," Uncle said not long after and pointed ahead to an opening in the forest. Water was as far as I could see. I had never seen water dance before or be so tall. I couldn't see where the water began or where it was going.

"Why does it dance like that?" I asked.

"Those are waves."

"Is that the Nile?"

He shook his head. "No, this is just a channel, but we are close. There is a lot of flooding here. I want you to stay put while I take our belongings over first." He readjusted the blankets and cooking stuff around his shoulders.

My stomach jumped inside me. "We're going to cross that?"

"Yes," he said and pointed to what he explained was a narrower section of the channel called Dhiam-dhiam. But it didn't look so narrow, since I couldn't see the other side.

I backed up and shook my head. No way was I going into the loud, crashing, dancing water that had no end. "No! I'm not going in there. I want to go home!"

"Rebecca, remember the soldiers were shooting at us. We can't go back. The only way to be safe is to cross."

I looked at Atong. She looked as scared as I felt, which brought me no comfort. But she said nothing.

Uncle took my shoulders gently and turned me to face him. "Look at me, Rebecca. I will take our things to the other side and I will come back to get you. I promise you'll be okay."

I slowly nodded, even though I didn't believe him.

He adjusted the blankets and the few items we had with us, then he and Mama Adau waded into the water. Soon their legs disappeared as they awkwardly began crossing, the waves crashing into them. Next their waists were gone and soon they disappeared completely. Just as I couldn't see the other side, I could no longer see them.

Atong and I grabbed each other's hands. I scanned the water, waiting for Uncle to reappear. As I kept my eyes focused on the spot where I last saw Uncle, the water continued to dance, but the wind picked up and the water seemed to get louder and bigger.

"There he is!" Atong yelled and pointed at a spot way out in the water. Soon, Uncle's head came into focus and his body grew larger as he moved closer toward us. I exhaled a huge sigh of relief; he was okay. But then I held my breath again—I was next.

"Rebecca, Atong, take my hands and hold on tight." I grabbed his hand and turned toward Mama Yar and my cousin. He told them he would come back for them next.

As soon as we stepped into the dancing water, it smacked me with force and my legs almost gave out beneath me. Deeper into the water we moved, as the waves kept hitting and tripping me. Just as one wave came another came right behind it, and soon I found my feet unable to touch the bottom. I tried to throw my other hand around his arm, but just as I moved it, a wave crashed into us. As my uncle jumped up and over it, I lost my grip and slid completely into the water. The waves pushed my body down to the earth. I couldn't breathe as the water rushed over and around me. I flailed my arms trying to find my uncle, but all I felt was water.

Somehow I thrashed enough to get myself to the surface where I gulped air and yelled, but under I went again as another wave hit me. My body felt like one of the rags Kokok waved around to get rid of insects from our hut. Back and forth the water pushed and pulled at me.

Just as another wave came, strong hands reached down, grabbed me, and lifted me out of the water. I choked on the air, terrified that Uncle would let me slip under again. But he held me tight and pushed his way through until we made it to the other side. Once I was on land again, he put me down, but still I clung to him. I was glad he'd saved me, but he had to go back out into the water to get Mama Yar and my cousin, who were waiting on the other side.

"You're okay now," Uncle told me. "I got you." His voice sounded strong, but his face looked afraid.

Atong threw her arms around me and hugged me. "You disappeared in the water!"

Uncle told us to stay with Mama Adau and not move, that he would be right back. We could sit and rest while he went back to fetch Mama Yar and my cousin. Just as he was ready to enter the water, he looked off to his side and stopped. "No, it is not good to cross right now." He pointed down the bank not far from us. The ugliest-looking animal lay on the bank. It had a squat body with four short legs, a pointy snout, and the longest tail I'd ever seen.

"A crocodile," Uncle said.

I'd heard about crocodiles. They lived along the Nile and could rip a person to shreds. The thought that I'd been stuck in the water with a crocodile nearby made my terror return. I started to cry.

He waited a while until the crocodile moved away from the water, then he told us again to stay safe as he reentered the river.

Just as before, I watched Uncle move slowly across until I could see him no more, and then I looked to the bank where the crocodile had been. I hoped it didn't come back.

I looked down at my feet. They were blistered and sore. They were also now bare. I'd lost my sandals in the water. Although my sandals had offered only slight protection from the rough and jutted ground, they were better than what I had now. No shoes, no protection. And still a long way to walk to get to wherever we were going.

I hope Kokok brings me extra shoes when she comes, I thought.

Soon Uncle made his way across with Mama Yar and my cousin.

Once we were all together again, Uncle took a spear he'd been walking with and went back down to the water. This time, he walked in up to his knees and held his spear high. He looked hard into the water, and soon he dropped his spear in and made a big splash. When he lifted his spear, a fish was on the end of it! My eyes grew wide at the wiggling fish and my stomach lurched, reminding me I hadn't eaten in a long time.

We ate the fish and began walking again. I sighed heavily. I was tired of walking. Shouldn't we be at the cattle camp already? Why was it taking so long? But when I asked Uncle, he told me we weren't going to the cattle camp, that it wouldn't be safe there.

I didn't understand. How was Kokok supposed to find us when she came? And where *were* we going then, if not to Toch, the cattle camp? But no one would say.

We hiked through more forest and grassland until the sun began to set. Just when we thought we would have to sleep on the ground under the stars, Uncle saw an abandoned hut ahead. I hoped nobody had died there; I didn't want to sleep among the dead.

But he said no one was there, so we could sleep inside, which would be good as the rains had returned. Mama Yar didn't cook that night. She pulled out dry desert-date kernels, mixed with some seeds Kokok had prepared for us, and divided it among us.

As the thunder and lightning crashed around us, I lay in the bare hut and wondered what was happening at home and why we couldn't go back. I didn't like the thunderstorms, and Kokok was always there to comfort me. No one would comfort me this night. I was scared, I was tired, and I was still hungry. Kokok had told me to be strong. I was six years old; it was time I acted more grown up and not be afraid. I hoped I wouldn't let her down.

🐾 🐾 🐾 🐾 🐾

The next morning we continued on. I stopped asking questions because nobody seemed to hear me, or if they did, they didn't know the answers. Sometime that morning we came across a village that Uncle said was all right to stop in. We saw other people who were traveling too, and Uncle talked with them. He told us they had heard an envoy was in Bortown, several days' walk from us, and that we should head there. The envoy would have food and clothing, which was good because we didn't have anything anymore. Our food was gone and the clothes on our backs were muddy and filthy.

On we walked, leaving behind our familiar villages and finding new ones. But these new ones were scary. Death was everywhere. Even the birds seemed to sense danger and quickly flew away as we approached. Clothing was strewn all over the ground. Huts were burned to the ground or barely standing. Trees close to the burned huts did not have leaves. There was food half eaten in the calabash—these people must not have known this was their last supper before tragedy came. Some calabashes were broken. There were still pots on the cooking stones. I even saw blood on the ground, but I saw no sign of life. But oh, the smell of the place! It smelled of fire ashes and rotting something. I'd never smelled anything so terrible. We all had to cover our noses to keep from breathing it in.

"Come," my uncle told us, turning us away from the villages and back toward the safety of the forest again.

We kept walking until it got dark, then we stopped in a clearing for the night. My stomach talked loudly, telling me it was hungry. But there was nothing to fill it. Crying did no good—that only seemed to make me hungrier. I was glad we stopped, because I no longer had the energy to keep walking.

"Uncle, what happened at the village where it smelled so bad?"

He looked at Mama Adau and Mama Yar and then sighed. "A fight, Rebecca. Those were the bodies of Jiech el Amer."

That name meant nothing to me. "What is Jiech el Amer?"

"That's the Red Army. Those were the boys taken to Ethiopia. When the army heard their home villages were being destroyed, they sent them back to fight. The problem is that those boys are too weak from traveling from Ethiopia back here. Many of them are just children—like you—and they don't know how to fight."

That made me sad. Boys, some my age, were fighting a war they didn't know how to fight.

Another several days passed, and each day was the same thing. We zigzagged through forest, grassland, and a few villages, always making our own road, but a road to where I didn't know. I just hoped we found food soon.

By about the fifth day, we stumbled into a village and saw it was abandoned just like the others. But in this one we found good things people had left behind in their rush. I saw sorghum, beans, and even clothing. I found some seeds, and Atong and I ate those. Then while my uncle and Mama Yar gathered things to take with us, I looked around a bit more. I couldn't believe it. Chickens! Someone had tied together a few chickens and left them, but they were still alive.

I need to take care of these! I thought. I grabbed them and ran toward my uncle with excitement. "Look, Uncle! I have *ajiith*—chickens! I am keeping them."

"No, you can't keep them," he told me. "They will make noise and the enemy will for sure find us and kill us."

I didn't care; I wanted to keep them, so I shook my head and held on tighter.

"Please leave them, Rebecca."

I shook my head again. "But, Uncle, they won't make noise. Please let me have—"

A loud gun blast came from nearby.

"Run!" My uncle grabbed my younger half sister and took off. I clutched my chickens and followed as fast as my legs would take me. We ran out of the village and deep into the forest. And even then we kept running. We didn't know if the soldiers had seen us or if they were shooting at someone else.

When we believed we were out of danger and we slowed down to catch our breath, Uncle checked to see that we were all there. He spotted the chickens I was still holding.

"You didn't obey me, but carried them with you, yeah?" he said. "Well, your punishment is that now you must carry them to Bortown."

"Where's that?"

"Half a day's walk."

Half a day didn't seem all that far after yesterday's long walk. "Okay, Uncle, I can do that."

"Understand that I won't carry them for you. And you can't ask Atong to carry them. This is your responsibility. And when you get tired of carrying them, you can't decide just to leave them somewhere so some wild animal will eat them."

"I understand." I was happy. At least for a little while.

They were heavy to carry! Atong offered to help me, which was kind of her. But even with her help, they still made my arms ache. Atong and I talked to them like they were people, our friends.

After that last village, Uncle told us we were not going to walk through the villages anymore. We would stick to walking in the forest and grasslands. Though the grasses were soaked with water, it would be safer, he told us. "The thick grasses will shelter us from the enemies." I was okay with that; I didn't want to see dead people anymore, lying on the road like animals. I overheard Uncle whisper to Mama Yar that he had seen people with their heads cut off or shot multiple times. They didn't know I heard them. I had never seen anyone without a head. And I didn't ever want to.

CHAPTER 6

The Sky Is Falling!

Bor, or Bortown, was much bigger than our village. That's where my mother's people were from. Our village was tucked away and peaceful; Bortown was busy with lots of people coming and going, and none of them seemed friendly or interested in helping us. We wandered around for a while, trying to find where the envoy was.

"Bor is not far from your mother's home village of Gak Adol in Kolnyang," Uncle told me. "We will wait for two days, and if the enemy doesn't follow us, we can go visit your mother's parents and relatives."

I didn't know anybody from my mom's side of the family, so the thought of meeting them excited me. I tried to remember my mother and what she looked like, but I could no longer remember. *Maybe if I meet her mother I can see Mama in her,* I thought.

Uncle located a newlywed couple who were related to us. The husband was an SPLA soldier. We stayed with them at their tin-roof house. The roof was shiny and I thought it was pretty. But it was so hot during the day, we had to go outside to cool off! And when it rained at night, the noise of the raindrops hitting the roof made it sound like it was constantly thundering outside. I hate thunder, so I couldn't sleep; I was too scared. And it made me miss our grass-roof hut.

After several days, Uncle finally found someone to tell him where the envoy was so we could get some food. We had to wait for hours in line with a lot of other people who had run from their villages too. I was surprised to see many older people waiting in line with us. As we waited I expected them to start singing and dancing in circles, like the elders did back home, but these elders just stood and waited. Nobody looked happy or laughed.

I was tired of feeling unhappy, so I looked into the sky where I saw a flock of birds dancing. "Atong, look!" I said. As the birds separated and came together again, I pointed and laughed. "This is a bird wedding! One side is for the bride and the other for the groom, just like people in our village do it." We giggled at the silliness of it.

When we finally got to the front of the line, a man handed us a bag of corn flour. Mama Yar cooked it that night.

I looked at my meal—it was paste in my bowl. "What is it?" I asked Mama Yar.

"Maize," she told me and dropped some into Uncle's bowl.

"This doesn't look like the maize back home." Back home our maize was colorful; this corn was white and colorless.

"That's because it is the UN's maize," she said.

"What does *UN* mean?"

"They are people who bring this tasteless maize. They are John Garang's friends."

My stomach jumped when I heard the name John Garang. He was the leader of the Sudan People's Liberation Army. I'd heard Baba talk about him and say he was a good man. Kokok called him John Garang de Mabior Atem. She said his name whenever she complained about why our men left our village to fight.

If this UN were friends with John Garang, I realized, our enemy Riek would want to kill us right here—just for eating this food. "Mama Yar, do we have to run again?"

"Why?"

"Now that we are eating John Garang's food, Riek will for sure kill us. Please let us not eat this food. I don't want to be killed."

"You will not be killed, Rebecca," she told me, sounding impatient. "Now eat."

I looked at the bowl again. It looked awful. I pushed my spoon around in it a couple of times and looked at Atong. She had eaten a bite and her face looked pinched.

"Why couldn't they give us maize from our village?" I asked.

"Stop asking all kinds of questions that nobody knows," she said. "You need to start eating this or you can die."

I looked down at my legs and arms. They were no longer chubby; they were skinny and bruised. So I took a bite. It tasted like it looked—bland and flavorless, with no ghee or milk in it. Even though I hadn't eaten much in days, I ate one spoonful of it and pushed my bowl away.

"This tastes bad," I said.

My uncle told me, "You have to eat it. That's what you will be eating for the rest of your life now."

"No," I insisted. "There's no green. There's no okra. There's no squash. There's nothing that my grandmother planted."

"You just have to eat this."

But I didn't want to eat it, so I didn't pick my spoon back up.

Uncle put down his bowl and grabbed my hand. "I need to show you something so you will understand how important it is to eat this tastless maize."

My hands in his hand, my little body followed him as he walked quickly down the road. I was out of breath because he was moving so fast. We were heading toward crowds, closer to where there was a long line of lorries. As we got close to the crowd, the people started to look different and scary—their skin looked gray and their eyes were sunk deep inside their head. Their arms and legs looked like *loch*, the skinny stick Kokok used to hold cows down. We went through that crowd until we came to a place where a lot of children were. They looked like ghosts—gray, with no fat on their bodies. Just bones jutting out of their skin. They had dead eyes above sunken cheeks.

"What are those, Uncle?"

"Those are children, Rebecca, just like you."

I covered my face. "Why do they look like that? Take me away from here!"

"No, you need to look at them, because if you don't

start eating that tasteless maize, you are going to look like them and you will die."

I removed my hands from my face and looked into the crowd of children again, my eyes locked with the eyes of some gray creature, squatting next to a tin of something dark. He put his hand into the tin and then brought it up to his lips and licked.

"What's he licking?" I asked, afraid to know. It looked like the cooking oil Kokok used, but darker.

"That's oil they use for the UN's trucks," Uncle told me. "You're going to end up like him and those other kids if you don't eat this tasteless food, because there is nothing else for us to eat. You just have to eat simple food for you to survive. But if you refuse, you're going to be like that kid."

I swallowed hard. I had seen how skinny my body had gotten over just the last few weeks, so I grabbed my uncle's hands and started crying. "I'll eat it. I promise!"

My uncle lifted me on his shoulders and we went back to our family. I was so afraid of looking like those children, I inhaled that food. That day after what I'd seen, the maize tasted like my kokok's cooking.

The next day, though, when I saw Mama Yar making the same maize for lunch, I couldn't bring myself to eat it. I cried that day because I was so hungry, but it tasted horrible and I wanted to eat something different. In the evening, it was the same thing, and again I wouldn't eat it.

That evening Uncle Machok left and was gone a long time. We didn't know where he'd gone, but after a while he returned, carrying a cup of milk. He didn't say where he found it, but he told Mama Yar to boil it for me. I had milk that night.

The next day the long line of lorries, or UN trucks, started their engines, as though they were going somewhere. Uncle Machok talked to someone from the UN and came back quickly, telling us we needed to leave with them. "They've heard that another wave of attacks are coming," he told Mama Yar. "They're taking people to the border of Sudan and Uganda in a couple of hours. Hurry and make the maize for the kids to eat."

Mama Adau ran out to get some water from the Nile to mix with our food. And Uncle turned to Atong and me. "We'll meet her at the lorries, but we must leave now."

Wait, I thought, *we can't leave now! We're supposed to go to my mother's village.* Did my uncle not remember? "No, Uncle, we can't go!" I told him. "I thought we were going to meet my grandparents because their village is near."

"We don't have time to go," he said. "Our enemies are near and this will be our only chance to travel without walking. Do you want to walk?"

I definitely didn't want to do more of that, so I shook my head.

"Then let's hurry up and go!"

I grabbed my ajiith, my chickens, and hurried after him. We raced to the lorries, but a lot of people were already there waiting and getting onto the trucks.

Someone told my uncle, "They're making us pay to go."

"What?" my uncle said. "They aren't supposed to do

that. They're supposed to be a humanitarian organization, not try to make money off of us."

The other man just shrugged.

My uncle sighed and rubbed his forehead hard. "We don't have any way to pay."

"Ask the driver if he'll take jewelry or clothes."

My uncle shook his head. "Our clothes have been taken. We have no jewelry."

"I don't think you'll be able to go. Sorry, my friend," the man said.

I looked at the line of people entering the lorries. It was getting shorter and the trucks were getting full. "What about my chickens?" I asked.

Giving them up wasn't something I wanted to do, but I could see how upset Uncle was that we wouldn't be able to ride to safety, and I didn't want to be stuck walking. My legs still hurt and my feet were still covered in blisters.

Uncle's face lit up. "Yes, let's try."

We got into the line and when we got to the front, I saw the UN driver and became afraid. He was light skinned.

I whispered to Atong, "I think he is Jalaba, Arab? Let's not get into this lorry; they'll kill us for sure."

"No," said Atong. "They would have already killed us if they were Jalaba."

The man demanded that we make payment for the trip. I held out the chickens, and he took them and let us board. The truck was long with no seats, just open space, and a domed top. It was already full, so we squeezed in as the driver closed the back tailgate behind us.

"Wait!" my uncle told the driver. "We're waiting for another person."

"No, we're leaving now," the driver said, his voice harsh.

"It's my wife. She's pregnant with our first baby. We can't leave her!" my uncle said.

"Then I guess you'll have to get off the truck. Either you stay on and we leave or you get off and we leave. Either way, we're leaving now."

My uncle groaned as we watched the driver walk from the back of the lorry. We heard him get into the driver's side and shut the door, then the truck started to move.

Uncle Machok sat on the floor for a moment with his eyes closed and his face pinched, as if he were in great pain. He exhaled heavily, sighed, and told us he'd get off at the next village and walk back to get Mama Adau.

But we drove for hours without stopping.

I wouldn't see my uncle's wife again for seven years.

❀ ❀ ❀ ❀ ❀

It was hot and dusty in the truck and we had no windows to let the air come in and cool us even a little. The muggy warmth, along with the bumpy rhythm of the truck, made me fall asleep. When I woke up, I heard whispering voices and people getting in and out of the lorry. It was dark outside. Someone said we were at a town called Torit. Someone also warned us not to talk because we were close to Juba, the capital city, and the Arabs were there. We were now in the middle of enemy-held land.

A stranger sitting next to me told me not to be afraid and then handed me a green round thing. I looked at Mama Yar and Uncle Machok and they told me to eat it.

"We won't eat for a while because we are heading to Kidepo," the stranger told me. "You'll like it. It's a mango. Good stuff."

I looked at Atong, who was eating hers, so I decided to give it a try. It was the sweetest thing I'd ever tasted. I ate and ate until my stomach ached. But then we were driving again and I fell back asleep.

The next time I awoke, it was morning and we were at Kidepo, a nice little village area that had a lot of grasslands and palm trees. In the distance I saw elephants, zebras, and giraffes wandering around. Uncle Machok said Kidepo was still safe from the war. The animals seemed to show me that was true—they were fat and beautiful. The people there seemed nice to us, but we didn't understand their language because we were from different tribes. This was the land of the Boya people.

We stayed there in a compound for a while. Atong and I played along the dried-up river, but we discovered if you dug in the sand, water would seep up from the ground. We watched the local people dig a lot so they and their live-stock would drink. We also ate a lot of palm fruits.

One day while Atong and I were playing, we came upon some bullets. A boy playing with us said he knew how to start a fire with a bullet.

"How, when you have no gun?" another boy asked him.

"You just need to move the top part and pour the seeds

out of the bullet. Let's collect some sticks and I'll show you. It will be fun!" he said.

I was curious to see him do this, because I'd never heard of making a fire from a bullet. So we all gathered sticks and put them in a pile.

One boy said, "Watch this!" and he began to rub two of the sticks together. Soon smoke came from the sticks and started a small fire.

I gasped! *Fire comes from two trees and from bullets too?* I thought.

The boy who found the bullets took one apart and poured black powder out of the bullet casing and onto the fire the other boy had started. When the powder hit the fire, the flames grew big.

"Ooh!" Atong and I both said and laughed. All the children made a circle around the fire and watched it.

"See? I told you it would be fun," the boy said. "Let's see how big the fire can get!"

"More! More!" we all told him.

He grabbed the other bullets, pried them open, and poured the black powder onto the fire.

The flames grew higher than we were! The heat from the fire was so hot we all moved the circle farther out.

Another boy grabbed a handful of the unopened bullets and threw them all on the fire. The bullets started buzzing and making loud noises, just like the sounds I heard the day our village was attacked. We began to run and dropped to the ground, covering our heads.

Sheeeeeee, the fire said, and then *boom!*

"Stay on the ground!" a boy said. "Don't move until all the bullets stop firing."

Another *sheeeeeee, boom!* And another, until finally the noise stopped. When I looked up, the fire was gone, just ashes were left.

The boy who first opened the bullets started to laugh at us. "Look at all of you, so scared like women!"

Once I realized we were safe, I started to laugh too. This was fun! So when the boy told us to look for more bullets, Atong and I joined in. But another, older boy said no, that someone could get hurt. Then they got into a fight, so we left.

That night I told Mama Yar about our adventure. I thought she would laugh and tell me how fun that sounded, but she looked serious at me and told me never to do that again. "People get hurt and die that way," she said. "Stay away from that, Rebecca."

Atong and I didn't play with those boys anymore.

Uncle said we couldn't stay in Kidepo much longer, that we needed to move on to Kapoeta, where we had some relatives. He kept looking for the UN lorries to show up again, but none did. He found a large truck they called a *glaba* that lifted up and dumped things out of its truck bed. We'd take that to Kapoeta, Uncle told us. It didn't look safe to ride in the back of it, but everyone seemed not to notice, so when Uncle lifted us onto it, we didn't argue. Before we left, SPLA soldiers joined our group. Uncle said they were there for our protection.

Even though the drive to Kapoeta wasn't long, I didn't like riding in the truck. The floor was covered with a tan powder and there were sheets of rust everywhere. Uncle said they used this truck to move building equipment. The back end was open and when the truck hit bumps or went up hills, people almost fell out! The soldiers were constantly grabbing people to keep them in the truck bed.

Uncle told us that some of our Dinka relatives lived in Kapoeta, so we could see them and stay with them for a while.

I liked that idea. *I bet they'll have good food for us to eat*, I thought.

I looked forward to getting to the village—until we got there. The people there were mean. They pointed and made comments about how dirty we were, how we didn't have any clothes, and how we were from the backward villages. Then the children started laughing at us. "Look at how skinny and sick they look," they said. "Look at *amuoi nuer bei Luak*!" That phrase meant that we were shut out from our cattle huts by the Nuer people.

I couldn't help that I was dirty and skinny. I had barely eaten in months. I looked down at myself and wanted to reject me too. I didn't have clothing on, and when I looked at Atong, I saw that she looked the same. I remembered before we left Bortown, Uncle and Mama Yar had taken Atong's and my dresses to make skirts for the women we met who didn't have clothing. Uncle said we were kids and we were fine without them, but it wasn't right for women not to have clothing to wear. Many of the women didn't have clothing, because it had either become too thin and useless from the long journey or because the soldiers had stolen it from them.

"Pay them no attention," Mama Yar told me about the people pointing and laughing at us. "They learn here the ways of the Toposa people, who are from this area. They cause trouble. They think they are of a better class of people than we are, just because we come from a different area of suffering. They will understand soon when they see *their* relatives arriving from villages."

I didn't understand why they looked down on us. I liked our village. The cattle huts were beautiful and peaceful and green. We had food all the time and as much milk as we wanted. We heard that in Ethiopia, a lot of people died from hunger and lack of water. But in our village, we had everything we needed.

We made our way through the crowd, and Uncle Machok started to talk to a tall man in a uniform. He was a general in the military and a Dinka.

The man asked our names and where we were from. Uncle listed his name to the tenth generation, because the Dinka name is very important to our people. They wanted to know who we were children of. Dinkas list the generations so we know who we belong to. As Uncle listed his names, I found myself silently listing mine. My first last name is my dad's name and then my dad's dad's name . . . and then I didn't know any more. In our village, I just said, "I am Rebecca Deng Awel," and no one asked me more questions.

The man Uncle talked to said, "We heard your village was attacked. Every time the UN brings people, everyone rushes to find out news. We heard people are being killed everywhere; we want to know who has made it out. But nobody knows who's making it and who isn't. Your family just arrived here two weeks ago from Ethiopia, because they have been attacked there too. They are staying at a compound not far from here. My guards will take you."

Baba is here! I thought. I wanted to run to see them— Baba, my stepmother Mama Atany, and my half brothers and half sister who had been born while they were in Ethiopia, but we'd heard about them. Atong and I looked at each other and giggled with excitement. "We're going to see Baba!" I said. "And you will get to see your mother!"

I asked Atong if she remembered what Baba looked like, and she said, "Just a big beard!"

I had the same thing in my mind, but I remembered how he smelled. I started to think about all the things I would tell him when I saw him—about how we had to run away from the gunfire and how I thought I'd been shot and how I almost drowned in the water.

Some soldiers escorted us on a short walk to the compound the man mentioned. Mama Atany was getting ready to cook, but as soon as she saw us, she burst into tears and ran to us. "My children, my children! Look at you! But oh, you're alive, you're alive! You're all here."

I looked everywhere for my dad, but I couldn't find him. "Where is Baba?" I asked her.

"He went back to the village once he heard that it had been attacked. He went to rescue you. He didn't know you had already left and were coming this way," she explained.

Baba *had* come to save us. But he hadn't come in time. I started to cry, just thinking about him. I hadn't seen him in so long, and now I'd missed seeing him again. Maybe he and Kokok would come find us together. That thought perked me up a bit.

Then my thoughts turned toward my oldest brothers. "Where are Luk and Padiet?" I liked my half brothers; I used to follow Luk around all the time.

"Padiet is here, but Luk is in another town called Narus, where a lot of other boys are hiding," she said. "Many of the young boys from our clan, just six or seven years old, ran away to Ethiopia to escape death or being forced to join the northern army. But with the attacks in that country, they had to come back."

She took Atong and me to a large green tub and filled it with water. She grabbed soap and began scrubbing our bodies. From head to toe, she scrubbed, then she rinsed us off. The water that ran onto the cement floor was rust colored. It took four basins of water for us to see the true color of the water running down our skin. She smiled as she washed away the weeks of dirt and mud caked on me. The water on my body felt so good, and as she scrubbed my arms and legs, I thought about Kokok. It made me miss my grandmother again.

Then Mama Atany took us into a room with a nice mat.

I hadn't seen a mat to sleep on since we'd left our village. She told us to sit on it while she brought out a jar of Vaseline and rubbed it all over our bodies. When she was finished, the jar was almost empty.

She opened a tin box and pulled out pretty floral dresses with matching underwear. We couldn't believe our eyes! They were so beautiful. Atong and I put them on, and as we marched out of the room, the children who hadn't wanted to be close to us started moving toward us. I understood why now—we looked human again.

Before we arrived, Mama Atany had gone to the market, so while she was cleaning us, some of the other women in the compound began to cook. The smells took me back to our village. They made *akop*, a type of couscous made from sorghum. I had long forgotten the taste of real food. Best of all, it wasn't made from the UN's corn flour.

Every day we ate well and felt loved. I enjoyed playing with my new brother Angong and baby sister Nyandhot, who were both born in heaven, what we called Ethiopia. I also had fun spending time with my brother Padiet, who had been at our village with Mama Atany, but who went with her, so I didn't remember him that well. I told him that when we were running from the village, I used to look at the stars at night and see all my family's faces there. They would smile back at me, and I would always tell Atong to join me in talking to them. When the sky was clear, their smiles were bright, but when it was cloudy, their faces faded away.

He said I was crazy, but he was happy we were "with them" through the stars.

We had a wonderful time, and soon I started to feel safe again. That lasted almost a month until we ran out of food.

One Sunday Uncle told us we had to travel back to Kidepo to get rice, corn, and beans there, because the UN wasn't handing out any in Kapoeta.

"Why aren't they?" I asked.

"Kapoeta is filled with SPLA soliders, and the UN doesn't feed soliders. They only feed civilians." I didn't want to ride the truck again, but I did look forward to seeing the beautiful palm trees and the animals. So we began walking back toward the UN truck stop on the other side of town. As we were walking in the town's center plaza, we heard a loud buzzing sound overhead.

Whoooo. Whoooo. Whoooo.

What is that sound? I wondered.

People started running in every direction and screaming. "Antonov! Antonov! Run to the kandak, the kandak! Run!" they shouted. I didn't know what an antonov or the kandak were, so I started running toward the nearest house. I turned to see where everyone else was, but they were all running in the opposite direction. Mama Atany grabbed my brother Padiet and Atong and pushed them down into something that looked like a hole.

Is that a kandak? I thought. I didn't understand these new Arabic words. We called things by Dinka names, plus we didn't have such holes where big people could go in like rats.

"Rebecca! Come back! Over here!" my family yelled. I turned and started running toward them, but something landed between the house and the kandak. I felt the ground shake and I froze!

The sound was so loud I couldn't hear anything else. I saw their hands waving to me from the kandak and telling me to get down, to get low to the ground, but I couldn't understand why they were not saying anything and only using their hands. More noises and large things fell from the sky all around me, but I couldn't move. I was so terrified, my feet refused to step anywhere. And I just kept seeing their hands pushing down toward the ground.

When the noise and shaking stopped, everybody rushed out of the hole and ran toward me. Mama Atany got to me first and grabbed me close to her. I could see she was crying and saying things with everybody, but for some reason I couldn't hear a sound. My siblings came close to me and were talking, but I couldn't hear them either. Why were they whispering? I got frustrated with them because they weren't talking in their normal voices.

Just because I didn't go to the kandak doesn't mean you can talk to me like I'm not normal, I thought.

While we were still standing there, a man came and started to clean the area. The ground was burned and black. Mama Atany led me back to the compound.

People kept whispering to me for the next several

hours. Later that afternoon, I felt ringing in my ears like a bell and my head ached. I finally realized people were not whispering; I just couldn't hear them. That made me dislike the Khartoum government even more. It took another week before I could hear people really well again.

They told me those noises and blasts came from Antonov bomber planes that flew over an area and dropped bombs from the sky. That day I learned those bombs killed some animals and three people at the marketplace. I could have been the fourth.

Mama Atany explained that the Antonov came every Sunday or during holidays when the Sudanese government knew that people gathered. They would bomb then so they could kill more people. She said the Toposa people, who were not with SPLA, told the Khartoum government the everyday activities of the town, so the bombers could come at the right times.

I couldn't understand who would do this to their own people. The Toposa people weren't nice, but they were still black like the Dinka. Everybody here in this city were all black people who were mistreated by the red people in Khartoum. But then I remembered when we ran from our village, it was not the red people who burned down our houses, stole our cows, and separated me from my beloved grandmother. It was people who shared the same skin color. Baba had said that the war is complicated. This was the first time I understood his meaning. For as long as I could remember, I had heard that the war was between us and the red people, but in my entire time of running, I had never seen red people (the Arabs from Khartoum). But I had seen their means of fighting—using black people and their tribes against one another. I also wondered why they didn't fight in person but from the sky by the Antonovs. Were we not worthy to be faced and killed? Maybe it was easier for them to kill from far away in the air.

That night Mama Yar, Mama Atany, and Uncle Machok had a meeting. After a long time they came back to us children and told us that in the morning Mama Atany, Atong, Nyanguom, and the boys were headed to Kidepo to stay. My half siblings would go with their mother. I wanted to go with them too, but because Uncle had promised Kokok that he would watch over me, I had to stay with him, and he didn't want to go where Mama Atany was heading. Mama Atany explained that Kapoeta was getting overcrowded from all the people coming from the villages and from Ethiopia. But the main reason was because of the constant bombings. "I'm tired of going and starting over and then two months later having to move again. We will move to Kidepo. We'll be safe there, plus it is green so I can farm."

Uncle Machok, Mama Yar, my cousin Nyanguor, and I were going to Narus, where Luk was. Narus was on the border and close to a town in Kenya called Lokichogio.

"Will bombs fall from the sky there?" I asked Uncle.

"No, it is safe there. That is why we are going. But we will have to walk."

More walking. And now I had to go without my sweet Atong. Who would I talk with? Who would hold my hand?

That night Atong and I clung to each other and sobbed. We couldn't understand why they wanted to separate us. When the boys and half of our family left for Ethiopia, Atong and I had stayed in the village. We had run together all this time. We had looked at the stars together and imagined our families far away. Now when I looked at the stars, I would have to imagine Atong far away too. I would be all alone.

CHAPTER 7

Left Behind

Uncle found us a ride to Narus in an SPLA jeep. I missed Atong terribly, but I looked forward to seeing my brother Luk and wondered what he looked like now. Uncle told me that Narus was where the SPLA and the Red Army lived. The Red Army, he explained, was made up entirely of children and teens. Some people called them the Lost Boys.

We weren't far from Narus when I began to feel sick. My head hurt and I was very hot. I had diarrhea and felt so tired I could barely move. Mama Yar felt my head and said I had a fever.

I can't remember much of the journey after that, so I don't know how I got to Narus, but once we arrived in the town, I remember meeting one of my other uncle's wives, Awuoi. She was a nurse and worked at the local clinic, but she didn't have any medicine to care for me. By then my body was covered with bumps and pimples, my fingernails turned yellow, and I hurt all over. My body felt like it was on fire. I thought my temperature was so high, I could cook a pot of food for eight people!

Mama Awuoi found a UN envoy in the area and registered us so we could get some tasteless maize powder. She wanted to find medical help for me, but there were no hospitals or doctors—she didn't know what else to do to help me.

In Narus, close to Mama Awuoi's tent where she was hosting us, they had boreholes, deep wells where the people could get water. By the borehole, the water dripped from people's containers and it made the ground close to the pump a little cooler. So Mama Yar carried me to one of the boreholes and laid me on the cool earth to try to get my temperature down.

Every day Mama Yar took me to the borehole, and while I was there, a woman named Aunty Aker Riak came to collect water for her family. When she got to me, she simply stepped over me and drew her water.

One day, Mama Awuoi, who worked with Aunty Riak's husband, asked him if they were aware that I was here from the village and that I was a distant relative of theirs. "She is very sick and we don't know if she will make it," Mama Awuoi said.

When Aunty Riak found out I was a niece, she said she felt terrible that she didn't know and that she had stepped over me every day at the borehole. So she and Mama Awuoi rushed to me and knelt beside me.

"I have passed this child every day!" she said. "I didn't want to pay attention, because of the nightmare of our lives right now with this war. Sometimes it's just too much." She looked into my eyes and began to cry. "She has her mother's eyes." She cried harder.

She picked me up and took me to a place in Narus where they had a few medicines. Her husband came toward me with a large needle.

"You'll feel better with this," he told me. It pinched, and I tried to fight him, but I was too weak.

I'm not sure how long it took, but slowly I began to feel better. The fever came down and the aching subsided. I was terribly weak from not eating for so long and not having an appetite.

I still hadn't seen Luk and I wanted to see him. But more than anything, I wanted to be in Kokok's arms. I wondered if she'd ever make it here and when we could go back home. I'd been sick and I had no one of my own to comfort me.

A week went by and one night we heard foxes crying, making odd sounds. People said the foxes were telling us that war was coming again. Listening to their stories of animals talking to people took my mind off how badly I missed my village and home. The stories were about animals singing or telling funny stories. I had never heard a story of an animal communicating about war, though. *Maybe animals in this area know only about war*, I thought. Two days later, I heard distant gunfire and cannons. A bad feeling came over me again and I froze. People began running around and packing things. A loud voice came over a speaker and told us that the soldiers had captured the town next to Narus, and we had to leave right away.

"What's going on?" I asked Uncle Machok.

He told me Kapoeta had been captured by the northern government and the enemies might be coming to capture Narus from the SPLA.

I was confused. Before our village was attacked, we were told we were fighting the Arabs, but it was the Nuer tribe or Riek who were enemies, and now the Arabs were capturing Kapoeta and Narus? This war and enemies didn't make any sense to me.

I was afraid and told my uncle to hurry because I didn't want to be caught in another fight like the one in our village where the bullets were like the mosquitoes of our rainy seasons.

We grabbed what we could—we didn't have that much to carry anyway—and set off on the main road out of Narus. The road was dusty, full of thorns and rocks and crowded with other people. Everyone was trying to get out of the town.

We kept bumping into people and animals on the road because we couldn't see that well. The night was black and the moon hid from us. I had trouble keeping up with Uncle and Mama Yar, and I kept tripping and falling. I still didn't feel completely well yet and hadn't eaten all that much, so my stomach ached.

"Keep up, Rebecca," Uncle told me. "I don't want to lose you in this crowd."

"Where are we going?" I asked.

"To Kenya. The UN is there."

"Won't our enemies catch up to us in Kenya?"

"No, they can't go there because it is another country."

"Another country?" I said. I didn't know what that meant. I thought Kenya was another village.

"Yes, this is Sudan, but when we leave Sudan, we will enter Kenya. It will be safe for us there."

On and on we walked and I started to get sleepy. Each step felt heavier and heavier. I wished Atong was with me because she would encourage us to keep walking. I missed how she and I would tell each other stories on our walk or play imagination games. I wondered if she was also running, since Kapoeta was between Narus and Kidepo.

"How much longer, Uncle?"

"They say it will take us a day and a half to get there."

"I can't walk anymore," I said. I felt sick again.

"You must, Rebecca. I cannot carry you."

"Okay," I said. But I couldn't.

Uncle took a piece of cloth and wrapped it around my arm and tied it to his waist so I would keep up. "This way I can feel if you fall asleep or trail off the road, okay?" he said.

I nodded and yawned.

We started walking again among all the other people headed the same way we were. But soon my feet tripped over themselves again and I struggled to stay awake.

My eyelids got heavier, my head dropped to my chest, and I fell asleep.

When I woke up, the sun was shining brightly over my head. Everyone I knew was gone. I'd been left behind.

🌸 🌸 🌸 🌸 🌸

I sat up, rubbed my eyes, and looked around. "Uncle?" I called. "Mama Yar?"

A woman I'd never seen before walked toward me.

"Uncle?" I called louder this time. But neither Uncle nor Mama Yar answered.

The woman squatted in front of me, just as my kokok had done before I left my village. "Come. I made food for my children," she said.

My heart started racing and I scooted away from her in terror. I didn't understand all her words, but I recognized her dialect. She was from the Nuer tribe—our neighboring tribe who fought us and chased us from our village.

The Nuer have captured me! I thought. *They have taken my family. Or they've killed them!* My eyes filled with tears. I knew Kokok told me to be strong, and I was trying, but everyone had left me!

I squeezed my eyes shut as she moved closer. Her hands wrapped around me and picked me up. She was very gentle, and her hands reminded me of my kokok's hands.

"It's okay," she said. "Don't be afraid. Come and eat with us." She grabbed a cup of water and offered it to me.

I was thirsty, but I didn't know if I could trust her. Had she done something to my family? Something moved behind her and I quickly looked that way. Two children, staring wide-eyed at me, moved. They seemed to look okay, so I took the water and drank. It tasted good on my parched throat.

After I emptied the cup, the woman smiled kindly and handed me a bowl. "Cham," she said, raising her hand to her mouth in a sign that I should eat. I recognized that word, since that was how we said it in my language. I looked into the bowl. *Oh no!* I thought. *It's that tasteless maize paste again.* She put her hand in the bowl and lifted the food to my lips. "Cham," she said again. I opened my mouth. I was so hungry, I forced it down. When she put her hand in the bowl again and fed me, I took the food easily.

"Where is your family?" she asked.

"I don't know." I rubbed at my wrist, remembering where Uncle had tied me to him. The rope must have somehow come undone and he didn't realize it.

She finished feeding me and gave me more water to drink. *She is kind*, I thought. *She won't hurt me.* I looked at her face and her dark, soft eyes. *Not all Nuer are bad like the ones who attacked our village.* I'd never realized that before. I couldn't lump them all into one group and call them all bad, because that wouldn't be true. This woman and her children were running away too. They had fled their village and had been in Narus when they learned the soldiers were coming. Her story surprised me. Her people had attacked my people, but they got attacked too. And I realized that she hadn't attacked my village. She'd had nothing to do with the conflict. Just as we hadn't. We were all scared and innocent, but we all had to run and leave our homes behind.

She told me because I'd lost my family, I could travel

with her and her children. That made me happy, even though I still wondered where Uncle had gone. We stayed under the shade of a tree until the sun started to go down, and then we walked again.

A lot of other people must have had the same idea, because the road became crowded again. At first as we walked, I had a lot of energy, but as the night got darker, I struggled to concentrate on staying on the road. I kept drifting onto the grass because the stones on the road hurt my feet.

I wonder where Uncle, Mama Yar, and Baby Nyanguor are. I wonder how they are doing. Do they know where I am and who I'm with?

The ground was dark, but as I looked to the sky, all the stars were shining brightly. I gazed at the stars and imagined I could see my sister Atong's face. She was smiling down on me and telling me to keep going. I tried, but my feet hurt badly and I was getting tired. I couldn't keep up with this new family, and soon other people pushed around us and got between us. My eyelids were getting too heavy.

I woke up again to see the sun shining. The woman and her children were long gone and another woman was standing over me and pulling at my arm. She didn't have any food or water with her, but she spoke my Dinka language.

"Come, we must walk quickly," she told me. "Let's go, they're getting closer."

I walked and walked, but I'd had nothing to eat or drink

and I felt too weak and tired. I tried to obey her, but the sun was hot, and the ground was rocky, sandy, and searing. The stones dug into my skin and my feet were bleeding and felt like they were on fire. I couldn't go on anymore and started to cry, but no tears came from my eyes. My throat started hurting too; it felt so dry.

I give up, I told myself. *I am not going to walk anymore.* I saw a little acacia tree, which some people also call a gum arabic, so I walked toward it to sit and rest and maybe eat some gum from it. A man saw me and ran toward me with a stick.

"Get up right now before I beat you!" he said, holding his stick in the air. "You'd better start walking, because if we leave you here, you will be eaten by animals or die of hunger and thirst." He brought his stick down on my head and I cringed with pain. I ran to get away from him, but the pain in my feet didn't let me get far. I was too hot and weak to run. Everything went dark as I fell to the ground and fainted.

I awoke to a hand touching my head and face. I slowly blinked my eyes. I was under a shade tree, and as the person came into view, I had to blink again. It was a woman and she had no color to her. She was whitish-pink, but not as white as our cotton in Kokok's garden. I'd never seen a *kwajaia*, a white person, before. She scared me because I didn't think she had skin. I tried to yell for someone to save me, but my throat was so dry nothing came out.

Though she was looking me over and talking to me, I couldn't understand a word she said.

"Is this heaven?" I asked her. "Am I dead? Are you an angel?" I had always imagined black angels and that my mother and sister Akon would be the first angels I would see, so seeing this angel made me feel confused.

She said something else and then put a cup up to my mouth and tried to get me to drink. It tasted sweet and salty and like blood, and stung as soon as it hit my throat. I coughed and spit it out, and it had blood in it. I thought my throat was so dry it must have been bleeding.

The woman placed the cup at my lips again and kept lifting it for me to drink. I tried to swallow, but it hurt too much. She wouldn't give up trying to get me to drink! As I was finally able to swallow it down, my throat started to feel better, and then my body felt cool.

She said something else and then lifted me into her arms. We headed toward a small truck parked nearby, which had other children in it. The truck was white, but not like her, and it had a red sign on it. I didn't know what the red sign meant.

She placed me in the back of the truck with the others. We fit in tightly, with some of the children sitting on top of other children. Then she drove us down the road in the same direction as the people walking. The truck's rocking made me sleepy, so I leaned my head against my chest and fell asleep.

The next time I woke up, a light-skinned black man was talking to me. I looked around and saw that I was still in the back of the truck. He said something, which I couldn't understand, and then he said something in Dinka. He asked who my relatives were!

I gave him my uncle's name. He nodded and said, "Okay, we will look for your family."

"Where am I?"

"You are in Kenya. This place is called Lokichogio."

Uncle told me we would be safe in Kenya, so I didn't have to worry about the soldiers. But what if this man didn't find my uncle? What if I was all alone again? And this time no one who was kind looked after me? As I waited, I looked around. Scattered among the people who looked like me were others who were much lighter and shorter than the Dinka people, so I knew this Kenya was a different place from where I'd come from. The land was much different too—dust and sand everywhere. Trucks and lorries passed by, rustling up the dirt so that it settled on everything in sight. I saw more trucks with the red signs bringing in more children, and big lorries brought in boxes and boxes of food. I scrunched my lips together. *It's probably all that terrible maize*, I thought.

Buzzing, loud airplanes kept flying low overhead, taking off and landing nearby. At first, I ducked down, afraid they were going to bomb us, but nobody seemed to be bothered by them.

I cringed at all the noise from the trucks and planes and people. It was so confusing and frightening and loud. I wasn't used to this much noise; our village had been quiet, without cars or airplanes.

I watched as some of the children's relatives arrived and

hugged and kissed them before taking them away. I wondered if Uncle was coming. More and more of the children in my truck left with their relatives, but nobody came for me.

Please, Uncle, come and find me quickly, I silently begged. I didn't want to stay here, especially by myself.

Just as I was ready to give up hope, after what felt like hours, I heard the familiar voice of my uncle. "Rebecca!" he shouted and threw open his arms for me. I raced into them, and hugged him tight. I'd never felt so relieved and happy in my life! He held me so tight I could hardly breathe. He cried and cried. "I thought I'd lost you," he said. "We made it that first night and have been looking for you for the past three days! I walked back and forth between Narus and Lokichogio looking for you. I thought you were dead! If you'd died from thirst, you'd be along the side of the road, but when I didn't find you there, I thought maybe an animal ate you." He hugged me tightly again and cried some more. "A worker from Save the Children or UNICEF found you. They had to give you hydration drinks to help you feel better. Oh, look at your lips, my child. They are so dry and cracked!"

I told him that when I drank the water the white woman gave me, my throat started to bleed and hurt.

"That is because you didn't have water for such a long time," he said.

I didn't understand the connection, but I trusted that everything was okay now.

He carried me to a field where tents of different colors

and sizes were set up as far as I could see. People were cooking outside their tents. "We stay in one of these," he explained.

As we wove through the tents I saw a huge tank where people were lined up to get water. In our village we never had to get in a line. Water was plentiful.

Mama Yar was cooking food outside our tent. "Oh!" She grabbed me in her arms and cried too, just as Uncle had done. "You're safe! We were so worried. Let's get you some food, baby."

That food was the maize paste again. This time I didn't care; I was too happy to be back with my family.

We stayed at the tents in Lokichogio, or what we called Loki, for a month. During the day we unzipped the tent flaps and stayed outside the tents, because they retained the heat and became suffocatingly hot. I tried to keep myself entertained, but there wasn't much to do other than sometimes pick wild red berries.

I wished I knew what we were doing here or how long we were staying. Most of all, I wondered where Kokok was. She'd said she would catch up to us. If she had the same trip we had, I worried that it might be too difficult for her or that she'd get hit by one of the bombs from the Antonov planes.

There was so much I didn't understand, so much that was confusing, but none of my relatives ever talked to me or explained things. I guess because I was only six years old. Of course when we were running from the village and I asked, "Why are we running? And why are people fighting? And why are people killing people?" Uncle and Mama Yar would just say, "We have to keep going." Or I asked, "When will we be there?" and they said, "We'll be there soon. It's nearby, in a couple hours." But those hours turned into weeks, months, and almost a year with no one saying where we were going or when exactly we would arrive. At first I was angry with them and thought they were lying to me. But as I spent day after day in this field with all the tents, I wondered if maybe they didn't know the answers either. I wondered if they were as frustrated about everything as I was.

One night while Mama Yar was cooking the maize paste, she complained, "If we don't move from this place soon, it will be hard to keep us alive. I am cooking white maize with frog's water." She meant that she had nothing to go in the water—no seasonings, salt, or oil, like we had back home. I knew the maize was *supposed* to be good for us, but I just couldn't get used to the taste—especially not when I knew what really good food tasted like! I missed eating the fresh vegetables from Kokok's garden, with the ghee and milk. I hadn't had milk or any fresh food for months.

"It's been a while now that we've been eating this way," Mama Yar said. "These children will end up being short and not tall like Dinka people. Their bodies are not going to have strong blood. This food lacks any real and good nutrition."

"Mama Yar, why can't the UN bring *our* maize to us?"
I asked her. It tasted wonderful and was so pretty with its
purple, blue, gold, red, and black colors.

"They just won't," she said. "They just keep giving us
this white maize."

"It is better than ours?"

She huffed. "The UN will not let people die, but they
will never take good care of us. One day, we will go back to
the village and you will eat all the good food from Kokok's
garden and our cows will have a lot of milk and ghee."

I looked forward to that day!

A few days later someone from the UN came and
announced that we needed to move again, because the
Kenyan government didn't want refugees at the border.
We were moving deeper into their country, to a place
called Kakuma.

"What's Kakuma?" I asked Uncle.

"A refugee camp," Uncle told me.

"What's a refugee camp?"

"A place where they send refugees to live."

"Why are we going there?" I asked.

"Because we are refugees," Uncle said.

"What are refugees?" I asked.

"No more questions, Rebecca," he said.

I wondered again if he grew tired of answering my
questions because he didn't know either. "I know my name
is Rebecca Ajueny Deng Awel. I am not a refugee," I said
under my breath. We were leaving another place, and just

after I'd found delicious *apor*, red berries, in the nearby bushes.

Once again we packed our few belongings and waited our turn for the lorries to take us to our new home. It was December 1991. I was seven years old now.

Part Three

Stuck

Marrying a girl young, often to a much older man, is a sure way to inflict poverty and inequality in her community. But there is an alternative: to end this cycle is to free a girl to be safe and healthy—to let her flourish and become who she wants to be, on her own terms.

—Desmond Tutu

Traditions were made by people; they can be changed by people.

—Graça Machel

CHAPTER 8

A New Place to Settle

We were in one of the first lorries to enter Kakuma. The people running this camp were from the United Nations High Commissioner for Refugees (UNHCR) and the Kenyan government. They made it sound like this place was going to meet all our needs. As soon as I saw Kakuma, though, I wished desperately I could close my eyes and open them to find myself back at home. When we stepped out of the lorry, a storm of sand greeted us. My eyes stung and my skin felt like a hedgehog's back. As far as the eye could see, there was no one single green thing on the ground or above. Uncle called it a desert.

My heart sank. *We are going to stay here?* I thought.

Everything in the camp was disorganized and people wandered around, not sure where to go or stay. I'd never heard so many dialects; we were all mixed together.

We finally found UN people handing out food and blankets.

This is it? I thought. *We're sleeping outside in this sand with just a blanket?*

The first night was horrible. Mama Yar tried to cook, but the winds brought the sand into the pot. Sand was everywhere, blowing freely around. We ate our maize paste dinner and every time I bit down, I felt a crunch on my teeth.

I went to bed only to wake up in the middle of the night with part of my body buried in the sand. I rolled out of it and dusted off as best I could before falling back asleep.

We had no place to go to the bathroom, so we had to walk across a dry riverbed to the other side and go. There were no trees or anything to shield us. I was embarrassed to have to do my business where everyone could see me.

After a week, a man, who was the leader of the refugee camp, assigned everyone to people groups. He divided the camp into zones. Within each zone, each tribe or a clan made up a group, and within that group were people everywhere. We were placed in zone three, group thirty-two. These were the Dinka tribe, and group thirty-two was from my father's side of the family. I was glad to be with people who spoke my language. I couldn't imagine living among all the other tribes or Dinkas with different dialects and never knowing what they were saying.

Weeks went by until the UN distributed tents to every family. The sun was so hot that when we were in the tent, we dripped in sweat. But we couldn't stay outside all the time because of the sandstorms. They shook the tents and the sand came in through the openings at the zippers. The UN people told us the land was in a drought, but when the rains came, it would be better. I didn't want to stay long enough to see if they were telling the truth or not.

I hated it here. There were no breezes, just stale, stagnant air that hung over the camp like death. This place was so dry the only thing that made it wet was the sweat from people and the tears from their crying. This place had no color to it. Back home, our village was filled with every color I could imagine. But here, everything was brown, lifeless, even lacking animals. No birds, frogs, butterflies, or even snakes. The one animal that was here I hoped I'd never see: the *manachol*, scorpion. I heard a woman crying and telling Mama Yar that one of her family members died from being stung by one.

Day after day passed, and the only thing everyone seemed to talk about was going back to Sudan. "One day we will go back to our village and start growing a lot of food. We will eat meat and drink milk," they said. I liked that thought. Even the town where we got bombed wasn't as bad as this place. At least it had been green there. And the dangerous places at least had mangos. We were safe here, but we had no joy and very little food or shelter.

I thought a lot about Kokok and loved to hear Uncle say that before long we would return to our village. "We will leave this dry place that is cursed with no rain," my uncle said. "As soon as the SPLA wins the war, we will go back."

"And Kokok will be waiting for me," I told him. By now, I was sure she was staying back at the village and not coming here. It was too hard a journey to take. She was back home, growing our food and fixing our hut so when we returned everything would be just as it was.

I also missed Atong and Nyanguom. I had no one to play with or talk to. Mama Yar was too busy cooking and my cousin Nyanguor was just a baby.

"Do you know how my sisters are doing?" I asked Uncle one day when I was especially missing them.

"They are doing well," he told me.

That made me happy for them, but miserable for me. *Why couldn't I have gone with them?* I wondered. That night I cried for hours in the tent and when my eyes held no more tears, I went outside and looked up at the stars to see my sisters' faces.

At night under the stars was the only time I felt happy, when I could look at my loved ones' faces and talk to them.

As the weeks became months and the months became a year and then two and then three, the talk about going home lessened, and life became worse for us.

The UNHCR continued to provide food rations, but barely. Every fifteen days they brought bags of wheat flour or corn flour, sometimes millet and sorghum, to the camp's distribution center. On those days we walked to the center to wait in a line that had barbed-wire fencing on both sides to keep us in a straight line and from cutting in front of others. It felt more like we were animals than people. We waited for several hours before they started to hand out the food. We had a burlap bag and a UN identification card, which we had to show to get our food. Each person in the camp received the same ration. When we got to the front of the line, local people from the camp who worked for the UN, who were called scoopers, dropped a scoop of the flour in our bags. Then we moved to the next station, where they handed us a glass of cooking oil.

Mama Yar said quietly after we walked through a line,

"No wonder things don't change for better around here. The UN people are not here to witness the walking skeletons we've all become."

Every time we received our food ration, Mama Yar would complain about it. "How can we possibly feed our family for fifteen days on this?" We had to spread it out and combine it with other family members' to make it last. Or we ate as little as possible.

Sometimes we had black days. That was when our food was gone before the next ration. On those days we drank water only.

We still had no bathrooms or sewage systems, so everyone continued to use the field on the other side of the dry riverbed. Sometimes, especially at night, we couldn't see where we were walking and would step in it. During the day, we would try to walk farther out where fewer people had gone. But with eight thousand people in the camp, it became more difficult to stay clean.

The Turkana people, the locals, didn't like that we were crossing the riverbed and using their land, so sometimes we heard gunshots; they were shooting at us to make us stay away. Mama Yar always complained that the UNHCR hadn't prepared the camp better for us.

Uncle called this the land of paranoia. Fear was everywhere in the new environment. The local people didn't trust the refugees, and the refugees didn't trust them. We could die from starvation or be killed—that was how everybody began to see life. It was as though everyone simply waited for their turn to die, like being on a life machine—not living but not dying. Every day life was the same. In the morning, we got up and brushed off all the sand that had entered the tent during the night. We went to the borehole, pumped water, and carried it back to our tent. Sometimes the adults sent the kids out to try to find and collect firewood. Then Mama Yar made us porridge or the corn maize and we would each get half a cupful to eat, if we had enough food. After our meal, sometimes we'd visit other relatives in other groups. I loved visiting my mother's people in group seventeen. I'd never met any of them before, but it felt good to have someone close by who was connected to my mother. They told me stories about her, and that made me feel close to her again. They told me she was very beautiful and worth one hundred cows for anyone who wanted to marry her. I hoped one day I would be as beautiful as she was. If we weren't visiting relatives or friends, we just sat around or played until it got too dark.

Three or four years into our stay, everyone began to realize we weren't going back to Sudan anytime soon. Fortunately, the rains came after a yearlong drought—and with it, life started to return slowly to Kakuma. Birds showed up and trees called *baygu* appeared. These trees were helpful for two things. One, during the black days when our ration food was eaten, the other children and I would go and eat the seeds, which were a bit like a bitter tamarind pod. Most of them grew around the boreholes. The seeds were so bitter that it was good to have water nearby so we could drink and wash the taste out of our mouths. Pretty soon, we'd be full and would go back to playing. After that, we couldn't care less about the black days. The second good thing about baygu trees was that we could use them as a building material. By now our tents were worn out, so the men took the dirt from around the boreholes and the riverbed, mixed it with water, and built huts. They used the trees for the hut roofs and for fencing around the compound. By now too, people had turned violent—different groups fighting each other, tribe against tribe and clan against clan. People would come in the middle of the night to try to rape the children and women or steal food. Because of that, Uncle often stayed outside our tent at night to protect us.

When we got too hungry and there weren't enough seeds, we would grab some of the dry mud off the huts and eat it. At first I wasn't sure about eating dirt, but I saw some of the other children eat it, drink water, and then have more energy. So I tried it too. It wasn't so bad and I felt good after that—good enough to go and play.

Even with the rations, seeds, and dirt, I just couldn't get enough to eat. By now, I'd started kindergarten, because the UNHCR opened a school for refugee kids. Every day the teacher gave us BP5 bars, which tasted sweet. She said it was for starving people who needed emergency nutrition so that we didn't get malnourished.

Sometimes instead of eating the bars right away, I would take them with me. I soon discovered that wasn't such a good idea. The older children would come and say, "Do I take it all or you divide it? You give me half and you keep half. Or I can just take it and beat you up." Sometimes I'd hand over half my bars, and cry. Other times, I'd refuse and fight back. But they were bigger and stronger, and hit me hard. They always took what they wanted. And I learned to eat my bars right away.

Every week the teacher weighed us. She said I was too far underweight, and told me I had to go to a place called the feeding center near group eight. One of my cousins, Akuot, walked me to the center, almost an hour by foot. The people there looked me over and weighed me again and then gave me a bowl of porridge, which they watched me eat, and fed me another BP5 bar. Then they told me to come back the next day. Every day after kindergarten, my cousin escorted me the hour to the feeding center so I could eat more porridge and the hour back to our group. After two weeks, they weighed me again to see how I was doing. I must have been okay, because they said I didn't need to go back.

At school we didn't have any supplies, so we all gathered under a tree and sang songs, which I enjoyed. Then the teacher taught us the English alphabet and numbers, which we wrote in the sand with our index fingers. I had trouble learning the awkward shapes of the letters, though, and felt embarrassed when the teacher pressed my index finger so hard to the soil that it started to hurt and the other children laughed at me. Once I got the hang of it, they graduated me to first grade, what we called class one.

In kindergarten all the kids were about my age, but in class one, there were older kids and even adults, since fighting in the war had kept them from learning.

Around the time we got the mud huts to live in, the UNHCR also built schools. Everyone was excited to sit at a real desk and watch the teacher write on a real blackboard. We even received our exercise books, pencils, and erasers. I didn't understand why the UNHCR didn't make the building bigger, since from the very first day our classroom was so overcrowded that not everyone could fit inside. Some students stood outside and watched the teacher through a window. I always got to class early so I would have a seat.

I felt proud of myself that I had school materials—now people would know for sure that I was a student. I loved learning. In addition to English, we learned math, arts and crafts, Swahili, and music. In art class we never had Play-Doh or any art materials, so we just looked at the pictures from a book our teacher had. In music class we never saw a piano or listened to recorded music. We just sang songs the teacher taught us. Sometimes we'd have a book of music that had black and white bars in it that the teacher called music notes. We had to learn those, because we'd have to name them when it came examination time. Soon I was best in the class. One boy wanted to beat me up because of it! He said there was no way a girl could be so smart, and that the teacher just gave me high marks because he felt sorry for me. I didn't pay any attention to him. I loved taking my tests and showing Uncle Machok and Mama Yar my handwriting and what I was learning.

Uncle decided since I was old enough to go to school and learn English, I also needed to know Dinka culture and our genealogy. So once a week, he taught me about our family line and history. "You need to know where our great-great-great-grandfathers and -mothers came from," he told me. "I expect you to memorize our family line back fifteen generations."

Fifteen generations? I thought and inwardly groaned. *I know only two!*

"And if you don't pass the test, you are not allowed to play. Understand?"

I sighed and nodded. I was determined to learn them as quickly as I could so I wouldn't get stuck with elders listening to their boring talks.

"What is your name?" he asked.

"My name is Rebecca Nyanwut de Deng de Awel de Luk de Ajang de Padiet de Ajang de . . ." I could only remember back seven generations.

"You are a girl from what tribe?"

"I am Dinka."

"From where?"

"I am a Hol girl."

He nodded. "What part of Hol?"

"Pathel."

"And which Pathel?"

"Pathel Thiei."

"What family?"

I paused. "Pan-Aluk? No, PanAjang."

"What is your immediate family?"

"Pan Awel Luk."

He nodded again. "Good girl," he said. "Now you can

go and play. You are getting better at remembering all of these."

I smiled and acted like I was excited to learn these things, but really, I hated these lessons. I didn't understand their meaning or importance. But if knowing them was the only way I'd be able to play and hang out with my friends, then I would learn them. So as I pumped water or stood in the ration line at the distribution center, I practiced the genealogy over and over in my head.

My uncle would tell me that every human being is a person and belongs when they are called by the name of their fathers. It is a beautiful thing when people know you by your father and you know that your dad is a very respected man in the community. Uncle always made sure to end our lesson by focusing on the fact that I was one of the first girls of this family line. There were seven boys in his family but no girls. How I turned out would affect the rest of the girls in our family.

I hated hearing that. *Why am I responsible for the behavior of all Pan Awel Luk girls?* I thought. *Some are living in Sudan and some are hiding from Riek Machar's soldiers in the villages on the River Nile's bank. How am I going to influence their behavior?*

"You must never bring shame on our family by being a loose girl or gossiping or stealing," he said.

I might not have liked the genealogy part, but I enjoyed when he and the other elders talked about our culture's artifacts. "One day you will receive a corset of many colors," he told me. Each generation has a dedicated color scheme, which explains a generation's name and meaning, based on themes and big events that happened during that time. How they got their name is based on how that year turned out. "This is how people get to know which generation they belong to when they are at the dancing ground. Each person will walk proudly wearing the corset representing their generation's colors."

Kakuma Refugee Camp had little color, so as my uncle described all the different colors, my mind went back to our village, to Kokok's house and our beautiful garden with its vast array of plants, birds, and bugs. I sat with my eyes closed listening to him and imagining the wonderful world we'd left behind.

We would go back, maybe not next week or next month, but we would go home soon. Everything would be as it was before the war. I was sure of it.

CHAPTER 9

A Ray of Hope

Are we ever going back to the village?" I was now eight years old and couldn't understand why we were still in this camp.

Uncle Machok looked sad by my questions. Finally, he shook his head. "No, Rebecca. There's not even a UN plane that can go there. It's too bad back home now. Everything has been set on fire. All the animals have disappeared and too many people have been killed. Nobody's farming even during the rainy season. There are no more seasons for people to farm, because they are getting attacked and killed. A lot of people are dying of starvation. Remember what Uncle Luk told us?"

Uncle Luk, Mama Yar's husband, had come, after he was injured in the war, and stayed for a while. He told us how bad it was back home, but I couldn't believe it. Not our village. It was peaceful, safe, and beautiful. Kokok was staying behind to clean it up. She'd said so.

"Can we just go back and see?" I said. "Just to be sure?"

"No, Rebecca."

"Well, is Kokok going to come to us?"

"Your grandmother can come to us, but we are not going back there. There's nothing to go back to."

My brother Luk told me the same thing when I asked him about it. He'd found us in the camp after we'd left Narus. He didn't stay with us, though, because he preferred to stay at the Red Army's group, where all the boys were staying. He visited our tent every now and then, and I often asked him those questions. But he didn't give answers I liked either. I was glad to have him around, though, and I would also ask if he knew anything about when Baba was coming.

"He is fighting," Luk would simply tell me and leave it at that.

Several months later, some of my friends and I were playing in the dry riverbed that we called the trash river, though its real name is the Tarach River. It is a seasonal river, and during rainy season a lot of children die in it. It was also our camp's toilet. There was all kinds of trash in it. We loved to play there to see what we could discover. A Chicago Bulls T-shirt, an I LOVE NEW YORK hat. Old shoes and broken glass. Or sometimes we would wrestle against each other to see who was strongest. We had a lot of fun at the trash river. When we were tired, we dug into the sand to find shiny gold, silver, and black bits.

One day as my friends and I were wandering through the trash heaps, chasing each other, and having a good time, a girl named Akuol ran toward us crying.

"Why are you crying?" I said.

"They just told us the names of people who were killed

back home," she said. "A lot of big people, like command-
ers, got killed. My uncle died. And Deng Awel."

My heart stopped. That was my baba's name. I stood
completely still, unable to breathe. *My dad? Dead?*

Another girl slapped her. "Why did you come and say
that name? That's Rebecca's dad. Why did you say that?"

As if all the waters of the Nile rushed over me, I began
to scream. I moved my legs as quickly as I could and ran.

It can't be true! I thought, my tears falling fast.

Just before I got to my hut, though, a neighbor lady saw
me crying and grabbed me. "You don't cry and go upset-
ting everybody," she said. "Your uncle's wife is very pregnant. If you go in there and cry, she might throw herself
down and kill the baby. So you better not show that you're
crying. Wipe your face and pretend like you didn't hear
anything."

I wiped my eyes and told her okay. Mama Yar was going
to have a baby. I didn't want to upset her and be the reason
she might lose it.

Dinner was ready when I walked in, but I didn't want to
eat. I just went to my mat, lay down, and turned my head
away from everybody to let my silent tears fall. None of my
family knew the news until the next afternoon when one of
my aunts came from group thirty-six. She was crying and
told Uncle Machok and Mama Yar about my baba.

The news spread quickly and people from our group
came with porridge so we didn't have to cook. Then they
sat and cried with us. In our culture when a person loses
somebody, people go to that person's compound or house

for weeks and stay with them. They cry with them and they wipe the person's face. They bring that person food and get their water.

People I'd never seen before came and told stories about Baba, what they remembered and liked about him. I loved listening to those stories. They'd tell something funny and we'd all laugh, and then the tears would come again.

I had my own stories too, but I kept them deep inside. I remembered his scratchy beard and how it tickled my face. I remembered how he loved to hold and hug me and how he brought me dresses and told me I was beautiful. I loved Baba. And I would never see him again. I tried hard to remember the last time I saw him, but the memories were fuzzy, since it had been so long ago.

For months I wandered around in a fog. Nothing brought me joy or made me smile. I felt like my whole world had collapsed in on me.

The names of the dead grew longer every week. At the late evening hours, instead of hearing dancing, singing, or laughter, the mourning voices would overtake the camp. People were receiving messages of a beloved one being killed. A majority of the dead were children, women, and the elderly. We heard often of men and young teenage boys killed, but the list of innocent exceeded the rest!

In the beginning when we heard all these names, I used to join the grieving families and cry with them to show support, but this had become an everyday task as more and more people learned of their loss. My eyes finally dried up and there was no more water coming down my cheeks, no matter how hard I tried to cry. I started to feel guilty and think I was not a good person because I didn't cry like I used to. I used to cry even when our cattle were given injections because I thought it hurt them or when cows had babies and made noise. Over time, when I heard voices of mourners, I ran away as fast as possible. It make my stomach nauseated and my head hurt.

When we heard of a relative's death, all the members of my family would throw themselves down and wail. I couldn't handle it anymore, so I would stay busy getting water. I think moving the borehole handle up and down to pump the water was a way to get my anger out and keep me from having to think about it.

Whenever I saw an elderly person from a different compound sitting with my uncle, I knew immediately that somebody from our family had died. Our neighbors, our friends, our family members—one by one they were killed either from the war or from starvation. I'd overhear the adults say, "That child died. Didn't make it out of the war."

And with each name of someone I knew, I felt more isolated and alone. At eight years old, my mind struggled to understand so much death and pain and the endless war that brought nothing but fear, heartache, and loss. I was sick of mourning and death and crying all the time. Just when I thought I couldn't feel more pain, word would come of someone else being killed and somehow my tears would flow again as my heart broke once more. No child should be that exposed to loss.

I began having a recurring dream in which I was attacked by an animal or some stranger. I tried to run but my legs wouldn't move. No matter what I did, the attacker got closer and closer. I tried to scream, but nobody heard my voice. Just before the attack, I'd jerk awake, breathing hard, my body covered with sweat.

Several months after I heard about Baba, one morning I noticed people around me whispering and I knew something was up. By the afternoon, when I got back from school, Uncle called me to him and told me to sit down.

He cleared his throat and wiped his face, but he wouldn't look at me.

I wondered if this had anything to do with all the whispering from earlier in the day. Still he didn't speak, he just sat in front of me and fidgeted. I glanced off to the side of him and noticed several people standing around, as though they were trying to listen to our conversation.

"You know the war is really bad and people are dying," he said finally.

"Yes, every week we hear of relatives who have died."

He breathed in deeply and then said with a weak voice, "Rebecca, Kokok passed away."

His words reached my brain, telling me that now I truly was an orphan, completely alone in the world. There would be no more talk of returning to the village. No more peaceful walks among Kokok's garden. No more wandering together to the pasture at sunset to watch the ostriches and all the beautiful sights there. No more being the pampered, loved little girl. This harsh, uncaring, colorless place, Kakuma, was now my home. I heard his words, but I had nothing else to give, no emotion, no tears, no feeling.

"That's it?" I said, looking him straight in the eyes.

His eyes narrowed and he looked at me as though I didn't understand what he'd just said. "Yeah... that's it."

"Okay. Thank you." I got up and walked away. And I never shed another tear.

❀ ❀ ❀ ❀ ❀

More violence rose up in and around the camp. The Turkana people grew angrier that refugees were settled in their area and terrorized those who entered their land. They killed a pastor in zone three, left a man paralyzed, and killed my friend's dad who lived near group forty-eight. When anybody crossed the dry riverbed to the other side to use the bathroom or try to collect firewood, the locals attacked them. The women, especially, were targeted and some were raped.

Fortunately, the men started digging pit latrines, so we no longer had to cross. It gave them something useful to do; otherwise they had no purpose, no goals.

As the war became more intense, new arrivals showed up every day. People who were shot or wounded and escaped moved into huts in the groups. When we first arrived to Kakuma, our group, thirty-two, was made up of a few hundred people. Now it had almost doubled in size. More people from other villages came. Refugees from other countries—Rwanda, Ethiopia, and Somalia—also came to the camp, and Kakuma became more and more crowded.

More crowds meant less food for everybody. And less food meant more violence. Crime seemed to be everywhere. People began bullying other people, stealing their food, and beating and raping them. These things were unheard of for my people before coming here. My language doesn't even have a word for *rape*.

Everybody complained to the UNHCR, but they did nothing. There was no place for us to go and find justice, no courts, nobody who cared.

One night while we were sleeping, a man crept into our hut to steal our sorghum and flour. Some of my cousins who slept in our hut with us woke up and beat him badly. I couldn't take it anymore and pleaded with them to stop. I'd seen enough violence. I didn't want it in our hut too.

But a few years later, violence almost came again to our hut. When I was about ten, again while we were sleeping, a man came. The group next to ours had had a party, so most of our boy cousins were there. It was really hot that night, so we decided to sleep in front of the hut to have a little breeze. The man slipped in and laid between me and a girl cousin of mine. One of my great-aunts who had come recently to the camp saw the man getting between us. She got up and yelled, "What are you doing to these children?"

The man jumped up and ran before she could catch him.

She lit a torch and examined my cousin and me. When I stood, my underwear flapped over and was hanging by a thread on the side. The thief had a razor with him and was cutting my underwear! She lectured my cousin and me that night never to sleep too soundly. "Girls don't sleep

126

like boys or dead people," she said. "You must keep one ear open while you sleep."

I was confused. "How can I sleep and stay awake at the same time?"

"You must learn. It is a skill every girl and woman should know. I will try to teach you."

After that Uncle asked Luk and Padiet to join our family. Padiet had come from a refugee camp in Sudan at the border of Uganda, where my sister Atong now lived.

Even my uncle became violent during these days. He lashed out at us or hit us for no understandable reason. Mama Yar said he was depressed. But I was depressed too, and I didn't beat up on people. "A lot of men are going through the same thing," she said. "In their villages they were providers or they had wealth. Now it's all gone and they are brought here where they can do nothing to provide for or protect their families. They don't even have weapons." I remembered when we first arrived at the camp, the UN people took my uncle's spear.

We no longer hunted, fished, or grew our own food. We had no work, no belongings. We could do nothing useful—and that affected everybody. Many people even stopped going to school. "What's the use?" they said. "We can't get jobs. No one will hire us in the towns. We have no paperwork and we are refugees, so no one will take a chance on us." We felt like prisoners.

"As people become more aimless, they turn to violence," Mama Yar told me.

I kept going to school, though—when Uncle would

let me. I needed something to break up the monotony of the days and give me hope for a better life than this camp could offer. I didn't know what that looked like anymore, but I knew someday I would get out of this place. I had to.

When I was twelve and starting in the fifth grade, the Turkana people killed one of the refugees, and the camp had been experiencing more and more attacks, so Mama Yar announced she was going back to Sudan—to Narus, where the SPLA soldiers were stationed. "Even in war, it's safer there than it is here. I do not trust this place."

"Take me with you!" I begged her.

I saw her eyes give pause but then she shook her head. "No, you must stay and take care of the men. There's nobody else to cook for your uncle and the others."

My jaw dropped. Mama Yar cooked and cared for twenty people every day—our family, as well as a number of male cousins who had come from soldiering in the war! How was I supposed to do that? I knew nothing about cooking.

"Why can't they just cook for themselves?" I said. "I have school."

"No, you are a young woman. You have a responsibility here now."

"That's not fair!" I said, anger rising in my chest. "The men do nothing while the women do all the work."

"Rebecca, hush! This is the way it is and you must do your best to cook well for them."

To pay for the trip, Mama Yar needed to sell a UN food ration card—something people often did when they wanted to leave the camp. They needed money to get back to Sudan, and people in the camp wanted more food than what was allotted to them, so the ration cards became very valuable. I'm not sure where people came up with the money in the first place to buy the cards, but somehow they did. Mama Yar couldn't sell her ration card, because it was a family ration card, which meant it allowed for four people's rations, and that would be devastating for us. So she opted to take my card, because it was an individual ration card. I didn't think much about it, because her ration card would cover me. I shrugged when she told me, feeling more upset that I was now responsible to feed all these people.

I resented being told I had to care for able-bodied people who could have cared for themselves. I was only twelve; they should have been caring for me so I could continue to go to school and play and just do my own chores—collecting firewood, getting water, and going to the distribution center to get our rations—not do everybody else's chores too. But nobody felt the same as I did. And just like that I was pulled out of school and expected to perform as well as Mama Yar.

The first meal I made looked awful. It tasted even worse.

"What is this?" Uncle said when I presented him with the maize porridge. He took a bite and spit it out. "Are you not a woman? Who will marry you with cooking like this? You're supposed to know how to make this correctly."

My meals never got much better.

129

For the next year, every day became the same: I woke up every morning and went to the borehole well to get our water. Most of the time there was a long line. Then I brought the water back to the cooking hut and I ground corn, millet, or whatever we had from that ration, and mixed it with the water to soak it. After it had soaked, I took it to a flat stone, where again I stood in line, to grind the corn on the stone until it turned into a paste (*guor*). There were only a few flat stones in our group, so the women had to wait in line to use them. After my turn, I looked for firewood in the woodless "forest," where I risked being chased or beaten by the native Kenyan people or by bad refugees. Then I had to figure out how to light the fire, since we didn't have matches or gasoline. I cooked the paste, making it into porridge or a kind of flat tortilla bread, so that everyone could eat something by noon. Then if we had enough food, I did it all again so we could eat in the evening. After we ate, I cleaned everything up. And then it started over again the next day.

I was terrible at this new routine, because the timing and planning for all these food processes were so important. I would often wake up late and then rush around to get things done. My hands were filled with blisters from pounding and grinding the corn. Often I grew weary of standing in line and would run off to play. But then I'd come back to find I'd missed my turn and had to go to the back of the line and wait all over again. The meals were often late, and Uncle would yell at me or beat me. But nobody lifted a finger to help!

I figured if I couldn't go to school, I should at least get a little time to myself to play, but Uncle didn't see it that way. He said I better learn to cook well or no man would ever want to marry me. He said my kokok started all of this, that she didn't even make me bring fire to our hut, which was a kid's job in the village. "Kids as young as two could bring fire, but you used to just cry when you were four years old and she wouldn't force it on you," he said. "You were spoiled."

Fortunately, after about six months, Mama Yar returned, saying Narus was just as bad. She bought someone else's ration card—an individual one made out to a Rebecca Reng—and gave it to me. "There. Now we're all good again," she said.

I was thrilled to see her, thinking I could go back to the way my life had been. But I didn't return to school right away. Uncle wanted Mama Yar to teach me how to cook properly, so I helped her.

As if I didn't have enough bad happening to me, one night when I was about thirteen, I needed to run from the cooking hut to our sleeping hut. It was late, was pitch-black out, and had just rained. I shoved my feet into my first new pair of plastic shoes that Mama Yar brought me from Sudan and immediately felt an intense sting on one of my feet. I threw off the shoe and began screaming, "Something hurt me!"

I'd never experienced that kind of pain before—not even the time when I thought I'd been shot. I got back to the sleeping hut and Mama Yar looked at it. My toes were already beginning to swell.

"I think a snake bit me," I told her, gritting my teeth to keep from screaming again.

We didn't have anything in the hut to care for it, not like we would have back in the village. So my uncle and a cousin took a blanket, tied it to two sticks, and carried me to the refugee hospital, which was near group eight. It took more than thirty minutes to get there, and by then, my mouth had started foaming.

The nurse took one look at me and admitted me to the hospital. "You've been stung by a poisonous scorpion," she told me.

"Are you sure it wasn't a snake?" I wanted it to be a snake, since I knew a woman who had gotten stung by a scorpion and died. Her relatives said her death was agonizing.

"No, trust me, it was a scorpion."

My body felt like it had thousands of needles sticking into every bit of me. Using the bathroom was even worse. Somebody had to help me get out of the bed and walk and then each drop of urine was like a needle jabbing all the way out. Just to move—just to hear somebody *else* move!— was excruciating. I didn't want any noise. I didn't want anyone moving. I didn't want to pee. I didn't want to eat. My tongue was swollen.

For a week I laid on a bed and wished death to come swiftly. But slowly the pain eased until I was able to leave the hospital. I learned an important lesson, though. Never again would I jam my feet into shoes without first looking to see what might be in them.

The next year I started back to school. It was wonderful, because it was helping me find myself. I was learning to read and write English, and I quickly became a star pupil. The boys still harassed me about it. "Sure, education is important," they said, "but for boys and men. Not for girls like you. You'll be lucky if you finish before you get married."

"You just watch me," I told them. "I'm going to graduate one day from form four," which was what we called high school.

As much as I loved school, I found something else that brought me out of the despair I'd been living under for so many years, something that began to bring me hope. It was around Christmastime, and some people were drumming and singing as they walked through zone three to our group thirty-two. They sounded happy—and when I saw them, they looked happy. Something we hadn't experienced in years.

One of the singers caught my eye and smiled brightly. "We belong to a church here in zone three. Would you like to come?"

I remembered how much I loved going to the little church in our village and how we sang songs and heard about God's great love for us. "Yes," I said without hesitation. "I would like to go too."

The next Sunday I walked thirty minutes to get to the church. It was just a few simple rows of raised mud for people to sit on with a fence around it, but it was filled with people who all seemed kind and happy!

We sang songs about Jesus in our Dinka language and we danced. They read the Bible to us. Everyone treated it as sacred because they had only that one Bible.

Then a man got up and spoke. He said, "This is the house of our Creator. The one who made us, all humanity, heaven, and earth. At this house you must come with a clean heart. If you have difficulties in your heart, you can ask the community of faith to pray for you. At your quiet time, pray to God also. Prayers are important because they clean the built-up dirt in your heart. Just like water is to clean dirty dishes and a broom to clean the dirty, sandy floors of our huts, prayer does the same to your heart."

I thought about his words. I could touch water and a broom and I could see their results, but how could that be with prayers? I couldn't touch or feel prayers and I couldn't touch my heart. I wished my heart was like my face so I could see in the mirror if it was clean or not after I prayed.

After his sermon, we prayed for God to bless us and help us be better people, and then we sang and danced some more.

I was hooked!

I loved that if I messed up a line of one of the songs, no one disciplined me. Uncle Machok beat me if I didn't remember our family line, but no one did that here. This was a happy place. I couldn't wait until the next Sunday to return.

Every Sunday I faithfully walked the thirty minutes to church to dance, sing, and learn about Jesus. I discovered that Jesus understood what we were going through because he had experienced pain, betrayal, loss, and violence. He offered up his life for us so we could live forever with him and never again experience war or suffering. We all had done things wrong that kept us far from God, but Jesus' sacrifice for us made us clean and holy before God.

I loved hearing those stories from the Bible and how much Jesus loved me. I needed to feel accepted and loved again. He did that for me—and he promised never to leave me. Everybody else had—my mom and dad and grandma, almost all my closest relatives. But I knew Jesus would stay true to his word and never leave me alone.

One Sunday a few months after I'd been attending services, one of the women asked me if I wanted to come on Tuesdays as well. I could beat the drum calling people to prayer for the women's prayer time. They prayed for refugee children, the war, and the changes they were seeing in so many people. Then they talked with one another about life and what they were going through. They were real; they didn't try to hide how they were suffering, and the other women comforted them. Those Tuesday nights became vital for me as I watched and listened to how these women cared for and about one another.

Wow, women go through a lot, and we have to be there for one another, I realized. I didn't know this was what authentic community looked like. I didn't have a mom, and my aunts and cousins didn't have time to tell me about growing up and life. But these women did.

I spent more and more time at church, feeling loved and accepted. Almost every day I headed there, where

I sang, danced, and praised the Lord with a clean heart. Where so much pain had been, he comforted me and reminded me that I was precious to him.

Uncle Machok began to grumble about how much time I spent there. "These Sunday and youth teachers are not that good. Most of them are men and they will not teach skills that girls need," he would say.

As I became more involved, he no longer wanted me to have anything to do with church. He told me I wasn't allowed to attend anymore and that if I did, he would beat me.

I didn't care what he would do to me, I wasn't going to give up church. I'd been forced from my village and away from my kokok, the person I loved more than anybody else; I'd been forced to live in this dump and eat food not fit for an animal. I'd even been forced to quit school and take care of him while Mama Yar was away. But I would not quit going to church—the one bright place in my life, the place that filled me with deep joy.

The next time I went to church, Uncle kept his word. He had a thin piece of wood ready to greet me when I returned and he used it on my back, legs, and arms. "This is for not listening to me. You don't go to church!"

The wood stung every place it landed. I cried but shook my head and declared, "Yes, I am going to go again tomorrow. You can beat me, but I'm not going to stop going to church because of you."

He told me I could go to church with him when he went. But the only time he went was at Christmas. I told him, "I can't wait twelve months to go to church for just that one day. With all the bad things happening, going to church every day and hearing how God loves me is healing for me."

So I kept going to church, and he kept beating me. I desperately wanted him to experience what I had found. His life would have been so much better! I wanted him to know about Jesus, just as I'd wanted Kokok to know. He could find such comfort, meaning, and purpose there. (When he saw how determined I was, he later gave up the beatings, although he still complained.)

At night as I'd lie on my mat and think about everything I'd been through, I'd say to God, "You are a good God, so why do these things happen to me?" When I went to church, God would answer my questions through the songs and through somebody reading the Bible, telling us how Jesus is a beloved Son of God but he was a person who suffered and was crucified. That helped my faith, to know that even God's most loved one could suffer the most too. So if his Son suffered like that, I didn't have an excuse to wonder, *Why do I suffer? You don't love me.* Because I knew he did.

CHAPTER 10

The Marriage Proposal

Blood was between my legs. I'd just come back from church and went to the pit latrine when I saw it.

What's wrong with me? I thought, feeling panic rise in my chest and bile in my throat. *I'm going to die!*

Frightened, I decided not to tell anyone. By the next day the blood was showing on the back of my dress. I'd gone to church that morning and, afterward, one of the women took me aside.

"Come here," she said. "Why are you walking around with blood on your dress?"

I inhaled sharply. She knew!

"You have to go and shower." She led me to a bathing area and told me to wash. "Does your uncle's wife know?"

"No," I said. "I'm afraid to talk to her." I didn't know what to tell Mama Yar—and what would she say back to me?

After I bathed, the woman gave me clean underwear. "You know how you sit if you're going to play?"

I nodded, feeling confused about why she was asking how I sat cross-legged.

"Sit that way and pull up your skirt so you kind of sit

bare. And if anything comes out, it will not show on your dress."

I avoided going home for a long time because I was afraid of having to tell Mama Yar. But the woman must have told her, because when I came home, Mama Yar had cut a piece of cloth for me. "You have to use this," she said. "You put it between your underwear and your body. Here." She handed me a small bar of soap that smelled like flowers from our village. "Go wash yourself."

I felt embarrassed, so I quickly said okay, grabbed it, and ran. At least I figured I wasn't going to die.

The next week, the woman at church took me aside again. "You know what happened last week?"

I nodded.

"You are a woman now." She pointed to a nearby hut where a mud wall was decorated with flowers and a small pole was sticking out of it. "You see that pole?"

"Yes. People were dancing there last week."

"They were dancing because that girl became a woman. When you become a woman, a man can marry you. So you must be disciplined and not play anymore."

I wasn't ready to become a woman. I didn't want to get married—I still had to finish school! How could I become a woman overnight like that, just because I started to bleed? I didn't understand.

On Tuesday nights the women began educating me on what it meant to become a woman. They'd tell me, "If a boy comes to you and says he likes you, you talk to him out in the open. Your body is the temple of God, and you need to keep yourself pure. When God brings your husband, he will choose a good one for you." Then they told me about how being a virgin is important in our Dinka culture.

One day not long after, Mama Yar handed me a beautiful waistband. I held it tenderly because it was so pretty with its intricate design of thousands of tiny brightly colored beads and its single tassel that hung down from it.

"I want you to have this special gift because you are a woman now." There was no clip to it. She placed it on me and then tied it closed.

I nodded, feeling the depth of being part of this long tradition of women who had worn such a beautiful piece of tribal connection. "Thank you."

There is a saying among my people that goes, "*Nya ku toch*." It means "The girl and a river" or "The girl is like a river." Just as the Nile has endless blessing year after year, generation after generation, so do the Dinka girls. It is a girl's job to bless society with children and her family with a wealth of cows in the form of a dowry. For a girl to bring a good number of cows, she must be a virgin and have a good heart to take care of her in-laws. They told me that purity was very important, because it would determine how I would be treated in my new family. Since everything in the community was connected and everyone knew everyone's business, there would be no place to hide. If the girl shared part of herself before marriage, everyone would know and it would bring scandal to herself and her family.

Sure enough, word got around that "Rebecca has become a

woman." Men began talking to my aunts and older girl cousins, telling them they were interested in me. Some of them were thirty years old!

When each suitor and his brothers showed up, my aunts and girl cousins talked to them, and if they approved of the man, they told the rest of my family. I didn't want to get married, which frustrated my uncle, because he felt I was being too stubborn. He thought I might have a secret lover from church or school.

Uncle told Luk and my boy cousins that it was now their job to make sure I behaved well.

Luk took his job seriously. He followed me everywhere and constantly asked who I was talking to when he saw me saying something to one of the schoolboys or someone at church.

"Nobody," I told him. "He is just a friend. I'm not interested in marrying him."

He told me I was not to have boy friends and that he was not doing a good job disciplining me. He started going through my school bag looking for "love notes" from boys he'd seen me talking to.

I didn't appreciate his interference in what little privacy I had or that he didn't believe or trust me. And I sure wasn't interested in receiving discipline from him! Finally, Luk told Uncle that I wasn't cooperating with tradition and continued to talk to boys. Uncle gave Luk permission to take me to a room and asked him to lock it from the inside so Luk could beat me and no one could come to my rescue. Luk smacked and hit me hard. It hurt! And

I wasn't doing anything wrong. Finally, I began to fight back. I grabbed his crotch and wouldn't let go.

Luk and the other boys learned an important lesson that day. Luk had been trying to demonstrate his masculinity by beating me and other girls in the family so we would know where we "belonged." Now they had to find new ways to make me behave.

Soon Luk went back to his old ways and tried bullying me again, so we got into another fight. He began hitting me, and I was bleeding everywhere. Somehow I grabbed a cooking stick and struck him in the forehead with it. Then he too started to bleed!

Some of my relatives ran to tend to him while I was left to soothe myself. "This girl is dangerous," I heard them say. "She needs more boys to beat her. A group beating!"

What they didn't know was that I did like a boy very much. I met him when I was playing with my friends, and I saw him whenever one of my aunts in a different group invited him over. In our culture, we don't date a boy alone; our aunts or girl cousins have to approve and they chaperone. Sometimes they spend more time with the boy than the girl does so they can study him for her. His name was Tongwut and he was just a few years older than me. He was tall and had beautiful chocolate skin, unlike my dark blue coloring, as they referred to people with darker skin. He taught me about how love is centered in respecting each other and telling the truth. I felt so comfortable around him and he made me laugh. Because he didn't have any dowry—in the Dinka culture, a girl's future family must pay a lot of cows in order for the boy to marry her—he couldn't approach my family to ask for me to become his wife. I told him I didn't care about the dowry. Sometimes, he would find an old magazine and pull out a photo of a couple getting married or a couple with their children. He would say, "One day, this will be us." And I would giggle in agreement. We were both orphaned but had strong families and relatives who would support us, he told me. I was so in love with him.

I didn't get to see Tongwut often, so we'd pass notes to each other through friends. Martin, a boy who told me he was one of Tongwut's classmates, started following me to the borehole area in the mornings.

"How are you doing today?" he'd say.

"I am doing good, thank you."

"I have a letter from your boyfriend, Tongwut."

I'd stop walking and turn quickly toward him. "Really? Give me the letter."

From that day on, whenever I heard footsteps while going to get water, my heart jumped with excitement! I couldn't wait to read another letter from my love. It was so easy this way and less risky than Tongwut trying to deliver letters personally, since my brothers would beat him if they caught us exchanging notes. I also wrote my response letters and gave them to Martin to take to Tongwut because he told me they were classmates at secondary school. The secrecy of my romance was exciting!

A year went by and I was now fourteen and had successfully fended off all the suitors who had approached my family. One day I returned home from school to find a group of men standing outside my hut. I didn't pay much attention as I dropped off my school things and started back out to play.

"We have visitors," my girl cousin said.

"Okay," I said as I rushed away to meet my friends.

When I returned later, Uncle Machok scolded me. "Why did you not stay to listen to them? Your cousin said you were rude to your visitors. They were here specifically for you."

I shrugged, uninterested.

"He has asked to marry you. He is not like one of those boys who will never ask to marry you or pay a dowry but is only interested in destroying a girl's reputation."

When the man returned, I looked him over. He had to have been at least thirty years old!

How does he even know me that he would want *to marry me?* I thought. "Uncle—"

"He doesn't have the dowry yet, so he's going back to Sudan to collect wealth from his sister's dowry who got married there." In my culture men don't just take a girl. They must pay something. But in the refugee camp, there's nothing to come up with, so the men must travel back to Sudan or to another country to find the dowry. "As soon as he gets it all," my uncle continued, "he'll return and you'll be married." Before I could utter a word of protest, he said, "It's done. Next week we will dance and he will leave a flag near our hut."

My jaw dropped. *What happened to my choice in this?*

The next weekend we held the Dinka traditional engagement dance and raised the flag he brought to let everyone know I got "booked," or engaged.

The next day at school, everyone already knew the news. The boys all snickered and said, "See, Rebecca? What did we tell you? All your smarts and you wouldn't graduate. You'd be married first."

"Shut up," I told them, desperately wishing I could escape. If I'd ever felt like a prisoner at Kakuma, the jail cells had just slammed shut.

"Rebecca," my teacher, Awilo, said. "I'd like to speak with you after school."

I didn't hear much of what Awilo taught that day because all I could think about was how Uncle had betrayed me, how I didn't want to marry this man, how I didn't want to have to quit school, and how I needed to explain all this to Tongwut. Perhaps Tongwut could do something, even though I knew that once the flag was up, I was as good as married. All suitors would stop coming, unless they wanted to pay a higher dowry.

"I heard the news," Awilo told me after school. "When is the wedding?"

"I don't know. He doesn't have the dowry yet, so he's leaving to earn it."

"Good. That gives us more time. I have something I'd like you to apply for. There's a boarding school outside Kakuma and they're offering scholarships. You're bright, Rebecca. I think you could win the scholarship and attend the school. You just need to write a letter explaining that you are a refugee and that your dream is to finish eighth grade."

I did as he instructed, hoping I'd be able to get away, but fearing my chances were slim, since too many others would also be applying. While I waited for the results, I continued to pass letters to Tongwut, knowing that now it was even more dangerous. He told me to be strong and that if worst came to worst, we would elope. But he strongly believed that God would find a way for me. He told me I was too young to get married and that he himself would like to wait a couple years to marry me, but if this man came back from Sudan, Tongwut and I would elope.

I was stunned when a few weeks later I got word that I'd won the scholarship. "Really?" I said, my lips turning up the biggest smile I'd worn in a while.

"Really!" Awilo told me, matching my smile with his own.

I raced home to tell Uncle Machok. I was excited by this opportunity, but afraid he'd dismiss it. "I'm going to school, not just a refugee school where teachers don't come most of the time and only high school graduates teach us, but a real Kenyan school," I told him.

He paused for a moment, as though thinking it over. "That's fine," he finally said.

In September 1999, I boarded a bus to leave Kakuma. This was my first time out of Kakuma since I entered in 1991. I would stay at the boarding school until Christmas break. The flag remained on my hut, but that was okay, because I felt free for the first time, even though I knew it was only temporary.

The boarding school was wonderful. Nothing fancy, but safe. And they had much better food there! The administrator placed me in sixth grade, and I determined to study hard. For that school term, I did better than I'd ever done before, and before I knew it the calendar said it was time for our Christmas break. I wished I could have stayed on this campus, but the whole school closed, so I had to return to Kakuma, where everything I'd hated about life was there to greet me—namely, that flag.

I hated even looking at it while I was home, and I avoided any talk that included my upcoming marriage to a man I'd spent a total of one hour with. I spent as much time at church as I could and I kept my focus on returning to boarding school.

"You aren't going back." Uncle Machok didn't even look at me when he said it one evening in early January.

"But, Uncle, I must! This scholarship is for two terms. I can't quit now."

"The man should be coming back for you at any time, so you need to be here when he arrives."

"I've had no say in any of this!" I stomped my feet into the sand, making dust swirl up around my ankles.

"No, not going to work, Rebecca," he said. "If you want, you can go to the other boarding school in downtown Kakuma. If they'll give you a scholarship, you can go there."

It was outside the refugee camp, so at least that was something. In January I began attending, but Uncle demanded that I work more at home to prepare me for becoming a wife. I was pumping and carrying water, grinding the food, and helping Mama Yar. Life became too stressful and intense to keep it all going, so I quit that school and returned to the school in the camp, going as often as I could.

It was difficult living in two worlds—one of unknown hope that education might provide a better life and one of a future already decided for me. I saw other girls who were booked have the same struggles, and they quit going to school altogether.

I was stuck. Every night before I fell asleep I poured out my heart to God, begging him to bring a miracle, to somehow change my life circumstances. When I fell asleep I had the same dream night after night. I was flying high in the sky and crossing a big body of water, so vast that it was all I could see in every direction. The wind rushed over my face and I felt light, without a care in the world. I flew for a long time, it seemed, but I didn't mind. I was having fun soaring and looking forward to what I knew was waiting for me once I landed on the other side of the water. Somehow I knew I was traveling to meet wonderful friends whom I hadn't met yet. I would stay with them and we would play together and have a good time. I would be free!

The dream seemed so real. But then daylight brought reality crashing back in on me—there *was* no escape.

Sometime in March, Awilo came to me again after

class. "Have you heard of this program that is going on for the Lost Boys and Lost Girls of Sudan?"

"No," I told him.

"The United States is taking some kids in to facilitate their education. One of the qualifications is that you really must want to go to school."

My eyes lit up for the first time in months. "I do, Teacher. You know I do!"

He smiled. "The second qualification is that you are an orphan. I know you don't have your mom and dad. Your uncle's family is raising you. And it's good that they have taken you in, but at the same time, this opportunity will give you a real chance at life outside of this place."

I nodded quickly. Yes, this was the answer to my prayers. God was listening.

I was now fifteen. I was much more of a woman and could be married, as many of my friends were doing. But as soon as they married, their lives became about feeding everybody and having babies. Most of them, who had been so beautiful, now walked barefoot in the "marketplace" with uncombed hair, looking hopeless as they tried to sell bread or make cheap alcohol to feed their babies.

I wanted more. Deep down I believed God created me for something more than just existing aimlessly with no purpose. *This could be my chance,* I thought, hope rising within me. *And this could also get me away from marrying a man I don't even know, who is twice my age.*

"I think it will be good for you to apply," Awilo said.

"Where do I go?"

"The UN compound."

My heart sank. "The UN compound? But that is far away, outside our camp. I have no way to get there."

He thought for a moment. "Come to school tomorrow during your regular school hours so no one will notice you are gone, and I will take you there."

I was so excited, I wanted to throw my arms around him and kiss him! But I knew that would get me a beating back home for sure! So I smiled instead. "Yes. Thank you."

I barely slept that night. My mind raced back and forth between the joy of leaving this place and the fears that the UN might not accept me. But they had to! I couldn't stay in this camp any longer, surrounded by filth, crime, and constant news of death and war.

The next morning I awoke early and helped Mama Yar get the water and pound the maize, as I always did. I didn't even mind doing it, I was too excited! I tried to act normal, but inside I was counting the minutes before I could leave for "school." If I acted too happy, they might ask questions, and I didn't want to raise suspicions. So I kept my face sober and my head down.

When my chores were finished, I grabbed my school-book. "I'm heading to school now!" I announced and raced out before Uncle could stop me with more chores.

My teacher was there to greet me as soon as I arrived. "Ready?" he said and led me to his bicycle.

I hopped onto the handlebars, while he took the seat, and off we went. We rode out of zone three, past the other zones, and out of the refugee camp, stopping every once in a while so I could rest my body and reposition myself. After two hours, we arrived at a nice-looking compound where they had greenery and swimming pools and clean buildings.

We found the building where I would apply. Inside was air-conditioned, and it felt cool against my hot, sweaty skin. I looked with wide eyes at my teacher. Neither of us had ever felt so cool in a building before! We both smiled at each other.

A guard directed us toward a room where we waited to meet with a lady to begin the application process. The woman had brown skin and was short. Her hair was braided neatly, and she wore a pretty blue skirt, white top, and black high heels. She was the most perfect-looking lady I had ever met. The best part about her was her smell. She smelled like flowers. I'd never smelled anybody so sweet before.

"What's your name?" she asked me and smiled as she looked at the UN identification card I'd handed her.

"Rebecca Ajueny Deng Awel."

The woman studied my ID card, then looked back at me. "This is the name on your UN identification card?"

"Oh!" I forgot it was a different card. "My uncle's wife sold it when she left. But she gave me this one when she returned to Kakuma."

"So you use this one?"

"Yes, this is a size-one-ration card. That lady's name is Rebecca A. Reng, R-e-n-g. And my last name is D-e-n-g. So just the one difference, but I am Rebecca too."

The lady put my card down on her desk and folded her hands. "This is a problem."

I swallowed hard and looked pleadingly at her. She held all the power and could crush my dreams with one word. I braced myself for the bad news.

"Okay, Rebecca," she said and began asking me other questions: Where did I come from. What happened to my parents. How far was I in school. Did I like it. Why did I like it. On and on I answered every question. At last she smiled and said, "We will just put you down as Rebecca Reng. Check the announcement board in your group in a couple of months. If your name is listed there, you need to return for a second interview."

I thanked her, and Awilo and I rode the two hours back to our group. On the way back, Awilo bought us lunch at an Ethiopian restaurant. I had my first *injera* there—it was so good! Awilo told me it was a flatbread made of sourdough. I loved its spongy texture and slightly tangy taste.

"My brothers and boy cousins come here sometimes to eat and watch a movie or learn boxing. Can I go see a movie?" I said.

"No, we'd better not, Rebecca. We might run into people who know you, and I will be in trouble because they might see you and me together and twist things around."

"Oh, yes, I understand."

I returned to my hut and acted as though nothing had happened. I was no longer sure how to feel. The interview seemed to have gone well and the lady appeared kind enough, but would the ration card mess up my one shot at getting out of here?

As the months went on, everybody seemed to know about the Lost Boys and Lost Girls program the UN was offering. Many of the kids were trying to get interviews, saying anything they could to get out of the camp. "Yes, I love school. Yes, I am an orphan"—even though they hadn't been to school for so long and some of their parents were alive and well and living in the huts with them. But I couldn't think about that. Instead I doubled up on my prayers, hoping God would give me this opportunity.

When the list was finally posted, people were running to check the names. No Rebecca Deng was on the list.

But Rebecca Reng was.

🐦 🐦 🐦 🐦 🐦

I began to see how the Bible was true. Our pastor at church often read Scripture to encourage us. One Scripture I loved was Romans 8:28: "We know that for those who love God all things work together for good, for those who are called according to his purpose." When Mama Yar bought a ration card that had the same first name, same first intial, and a one-letter difference on the last name, no one ever suspected how God might use that to allow me to apply to the UN program without my family knowing.

It was essential that they didn't know, because they would have forbidden me to go. Uncle would have forced me to stay and get married. My life would become meaningless, desperate. I knew God was showing me that he loved me—and that he had a purpose for me. Perhaps it was to make others aware of what war does to innocent people who are forced to become refugees. I didn't know, but a month later I gladly rode on my teacher's handlebars for two hours back to the UN building for my second interview—and several months after that, for my third interview, in which they did a medical checkup on me, drawing blood and testing me for any kind of disease. By this point, they'd collected paperwork and schoolwork showing that I was Rebecca A. Deng and hadn't left the camp but had been there since its opening in 1991/1992.

I dared to hope that all those years of waiting and longing to be free again might actually become a reality. The months passed as I waited to hear if I was accepted into the program. One night, I lay on my mat and began to think.

If I get picked, I'll be starting a new life in a new country where I speak only a few words of the language, but where everything will be different, foreign to me. It will be difficult to transition. Will I lose my Dinka culture and ways? Will I make friends there and succeed in school? Will they treat me as the Turkana people do, with disdain and anger? Will I still have to eat this awful flour paste? Will this new place be green and colorful and filled with joy and laughter? Will I be safe and far away from war? And then I realized, *I'll be all alone. Completely disconnected from my relatives who raised me and tried their best to teach me our ways, who taught me how to lift my head when things are difficult, who told me stories of my family and what proud people we are. Will I be okay all alone?*

I stopped thinking for a moment and looked up at the stars. I imagined Kokok's and Baba's faces there smiling down on me, as I had my whole life whenever I felt afraid or distant from my family. Then I looked at the whole sky, the great ocean above.

"The Creator of heaven and earth is with me," I whispered to the night air. "He sees me and he will be wherever I go, so, no, I won't be all alone. I will be just fine."

CHAPTER 11

At Long Last

The final list was on the board and everybody crowded around to see it. I scanned it until I came to my name.

It was there! I let out a joyful sigh as I read the rest of the announcement:

Accepted into the Lost Boys and Lost Girls Program... first group to resettle... November 5, 2000... United States... come for cultural orientation...

This was it, it was really happening! I would be in the first group of Lost Boys and Lost Girls to resettle to the United States. I reread the words, afraid I'd misread them. The date sunk into my mind—November 5. Two weeks away.

I jumped up and raced to find Awilo to share my joy. Halfway there, I stopped running. It hit me that my family had no idea what I'd done!

I should tell them, I thought. *What will they say? What will Uncle say?* I stood up straight, lifted my head high, and began to run again. *It doesn't matter what he says. If he loves me, he should know that I'm choosing a better life for myself.*

My teacher jumped up and down with me when I gave him the news. "Rebecca, you did it! You're such a bright young woman, nothing can hold you back. I'm proud of you!"

Now I had the hard job of telling my family. I hoped my uncle responded the same as my teacher.

When I got to the hut, Mama Yar was the only one there. "Mama Yar, I must speak with you." I told her everything—how I'd applied, the mix-up with the ration cards, and that I'd been accepted. Tears came to her eyes as she listened, but she said nothing until I finished.

"You must go, Rebecca. You must leave this place. We both know this is no place for women and children. The United States will be better for you." She wiped her tears and smiled. "Do not worry. I'll talk to your uncle. I don't know how he's going to take it, though. Or we can just try to do it on the down-low, and the day you leave, you pretend you're going to visit your mom's side of the family. Then you leave." She shook her head. "No, I'll say something."

That night after we ate, Mama Yar looked at me and nodded. I knew she was telling me to make myself scarce while she told my uncle. So I wandered around, praying and wondering how Uncle was taking it. When I could wander no more, I returned to our hut.

"Rebecca," Uncle Machok said. His voice didn't sound angry, so I took that as a good sign.

"Yes, Uncle?"

He beckoned me to sit on his lap, something he hadn't done since I was a little girl. I did as he asked and he put his arms around me and held me tightly. He didn't say anything for a while, but tears began to roll down his cheeks.

How can somebody who constantly beats you when you make a mistake love you so much at the same time? Then I realized that even though I was going to leave for freedom, he couldn't.

"I know there's a flag here and somebody has booked you for marriage for almost a year now, and he's still in Sudan working for your dowry. I know you don't want this. I raised you. You are like my child. I watched you as a little girl, and I know this desire to leave is going to keep alive in you. If we give you to this man, you're going to run away and it will break you. That is not my wish for you, Rebecca." He grew silent for a long moment, then finally said, "You are allowed to go to the United States."

My eyes opened wide. He'd said yes.

I threw my arms around him. "Thank you, Uncle! I'm going to go to school there. And everything I've always wanted to do, I will do those things."

He laughed. "I don't doubt that, Rebecca. You have a strong will." Then he looked directly into my eyes. "The spirit of your dad and your grandmother is with you. This is what your mother, dad, and kokok would wish for you."

He moved me off his lap and we stood. "I will talk to the rest of the family tomorrow about this good news and we will have prayers for you. I have a little money stashed away from my construction work, so I am going to buy a goat, and if the money is not enough, we can buy beef, onions, and cabbage, and we will bless you off for your journey."

I hugged him again. "Thank you, Uncle. This means so much to have your approval."

The next day, I found someone who was willing to give me a bicycle ride to the UN compound for cultural orientation. When I entered the room where the first group of Lost Boys and Lost Girls were gathering, I felt sad. Only a few other girls were there.

A person from the UN congratulated us and handed out books with the Statue of Liberty on the cover. It read, "Welcome to America." The book talked about the climate and how in some places it gets very cold. It also talked about different cultural aspects, such as that money is in dollars. It was difficult for me to understand all the things the book talked about.

He explained that for those of us who were underage, like me, we would live with foster families, who had already been picked out for us. He said that because we didn't have birth certificates, the US government would consider our birthdates to be January 1 of the approximate year we were born. One of my aunts had told me my birthday was December 6, 1985, but without an official birth certificate, my birthday would now be recognized on January 1, 1985.

The man told us that because the United States was so far away, it would take a long time to get there. We would fly on an airplane from Kakuma's airstrip to Nairobi, and from there we'd have a layover in Europe, then fly to New York City, and then disperse from there to our families.

We each received our city assignments. I was going to Grand Rapids, Michigan. I'd heard of Chicago, Miami, LA, and New York, but I'd never heard of this place called Grand Rapids. It frightened me because I thought the word *rapids* was *rubbish*, or garbage—Grand Rubbish.

They are taking me to a place of garbage dumps? I thought. I knew in places like Nairobi, stray children lived in the rubbish piles because they didn't have homes, but I was certain the United States wouldn't do that to refugee children. *No, they won't do that to me. I am a lucky person to go to the USA and I should not worry.*

At the end of our orientation, the man told us to return the following week for a final health examination. If we passed that, we were assured of a spot out of Kakuma.

My mind drifted to my recurring dream of flying over a large body of water. Had God been preparing me for this new adventure?

Over the next days everybody descended on my hut! They offered me advice and blessings, telling me to be good and to make them proud, and most of all, not to forget where I came from—the land of the proud Dinka people.

The women at my church held a special prayer meeting for me. They talked for hours, each one taking a turn.

"You are going now to be *abikok*, a foreigner, in a land that your grandfather never set foot in. You must keep yourself pure and stay strong. Lean on God for his strength to help you when it gets difficult," one woman told me.

"You know now about the suffering of your people;

please share that with them," another said. "Show that Dinka people are good people and that we have suffered so much from the Arabs. We have suffered much, but we are not bad people. We are people who just need to live in peace. Show them our tradition of respecting one another."

"Remember over in America nobody knows about your upbringing, so you must speak up for yourself," yet another woman told me. "Let your actions speak louder than your words."

But mostly I heard this over and over: "Make sure you marry a son of the land. Somebody who knows your family roots. Someone who knows you are the daughter of Deng Awel Luk. Find a Dinka husband when you are there."

I nodded over everything they said.

Time seemed to speed up and slow down all at once. It was going slowly as I continued to fetch water, help Mama Yar pound the food into flour and paste, and do the other chores, but it went quickly as I tried to visit as many friends and family as I could. I went to my mother's side of the family and spent time there. I continued to go to church, always praying that my foster family would be Christians who would take me to church in America. And I visited Tongwut. His church friends made lunch for me and my friend who accompanied me. They prayed for us. Tongwut said he was happy for me to go to the United States. He said if our love continued for each other, he might apply to go to the US too, since he was an orphan. That made me happy. I loved that we might both be in the US and might be free to be with each other.

A few days later I saw his classmate Martin following me. "I hear you are going to America?"

"Yes," I told him.

"Maybe I could come as your boyfriend? I like you a lot."

"I don't even know you. Besides, I already have a boyfriend," I said and walked quickly away. I was okay with him when he was passing notes between Tongwut and me, but several times he'd made moves on me or said things that made me uncomfortable, that he loved me and wanted to marry me—he even talked to one of my aunts about it! I shook off my thoughts of him. I had more important things to focus on.

The next week I got another bicycle ride from someone heading toward the UN compound and then I walked the rest of the way. At the compound, they had a tent set up for International Organization for Immigration (IOM), the group that was handling us. They checked my health and gave me a pregnancy test, an HIV/AIDS test—which we'd always called the "8 disease," because that was what we thought it was named—as well as other tests. Even though I'd passed them all the first time, with the trip now being a week away, they wanted to make sure I was still in good health.

Now the countdown began. One week out and the reality was starting to set in for our group thirty-two, but also for the rest of the camp. Rumors started about where we were really headed, rumors that terrified all of us.

"You know these children are not going to the United

States. They are going to Khartoum to become slaves for the Khartoum government," people whispered. "This is a trick of Omar al-Bashir." People began to believe that Bashir, the president of Sudan, hired people to act like they were part of the UN, and then the Lost Boys and Lost Girls would get on the plane, thinking they were going to the US, and instead would be flown to Khartoum to be killed or enslaved because we are the black people of John Garang de Mabior, seed of southern Sudan.

I was afraid too, but also confused. *If this is true*, I thought, *why did the UN try to protect us for eight years here and not just hand us over to the Khartoum government and be done with it?*

I began to rethink going, but then I was faced with the reality of the man I was to marry returning with a dowry. Uncle said he knew I would run away if I were forced to marry that man, but that was when I'd said yes to going to the United States. He might change his mind if I were to remain. *No*, I decided. *It is best for me to take my chances and leave. If I become a slave in Khartoum, it is better than being a slave here.*

I received word that I passed all my tests, so I returned to the UN compound for the last time before my flight, hitching a ride on someone's bicycle and then walking the rest of the way, to get our last-minute instructions. There they told us what time the flight left Kakuma's airstrip. They also told us that we could take nothing with us. But what did I have of value to take anyway? Everything had been stripped from me when I was forced from my village. This would be a fresh start in a land of great opportunity.

The next day my uncle did as he promised and bought

a goat for us to feast on. Many in our group were invited to celebrate. It was the best feast we'd had in the eight years I lived in Kakuma. We ate, we laughed, we danced. As we enjoyed ourselves, I looked at the love I saw on everybody's faces. My family loved me so much, they had all gathered to show me their support. They were trusting their God and ancestors to protect me on my journey to the unknown world, America! I thought for the first time of how Kakuma Refugee Camp was my loving community. We had celebrated World Refugee Day with other refugees. It was where I had learned about Dinka courtship and dancing. It was my playground with no bombs falling from the sky. I swallowed the lump in my throat as I looked around again.

Do I really want to go to the United States where I might not have people who love me? I wondered again. *We might be poor and illiterate, I get beaten by my uncle and brothers to "behave," but this is my family.* This was the family in which older people always gave the younger ones food to eat first before they ate. This was the family in which my brothers and cousins were there to protect me if outsiders came to hurt me. When there was fear in the camp, all the men in my family slept outside to protect us while the girls and women stayed inside. *I'm leaving this behind to search for an education and a better future? Perhaps I am crazy.*

Uncle Machok started talking about WunAjang, the nation of Ajang, referring to our great-great-grandfather, the founder of our clan. (This was also the nickname he often called me by.) Then he said, "I bless you to go to America and if this man who wanted to marry you comes back, your other uncles and I will give him a message of rejection. That man's family is a good family, but I know you don't want that. You go to America, my child. Remember all the advice your beloved family gave you. Think about them all the time."

❀ ❀ ❀ ❀ ❀

November 3, 2000, came—my last two days in Kakuma.

I awoke early, thinking how surreal it felt to be leaving the camp that had been my home for the past eight years. Well, not really a home—a place where I existed, but not my home. My home had been my village in Sudan. That would always be my home, but I hoped that America would become a new home to me.

I helped Mama Yar, as I always had, but I also spent final moments catching up with my family. My girl cousins asked me to leave them my clothes since I was allowed to take only one set of clothes with me. So later that morning, I went to the borehole to wash them so they would be nice and clean for my cousins.

Martin stopped by. "Rebecca, I have another letter for you."

"Okay, thank you," I said and took it from him, then went back to washing.

"I know you are leaving in two days. You are lucky."

"Yeah, I'm happy," I said.

"Hey, I really want to talk to you. Maybe you could—"

"No, I don't have time. I'm going to visit my brother's friend, Adam, this afternoon to say good-bye, and then I must finish getting ready to leave."

His face fell. "Oh, okay," he said and walked away.

I finished washing my clothes and took them back to our hut and hung them to dry. Then after lunch, I told Luk I was headed to Adam's hut.

I greeted Adam and we chatted a bit about my trip, and then he told me he was going to run to a nearby store to grab a Coke. He told me he'd be right back, so I nodded and said I'd wait.

Adam had barely left when Martin walked in, surprising me.

"Hi, Rebecca," he said and smiled.

Why is he here? What's going on? I immediately felt uneasy.

He turned and shut the door. Instinctively I backed away.

"What do you want?" I said.

"I know you don't like me. Your mind is on Tongwut." He stepped close to me and I could smell his hot breath.

I looked out the window and saw one of my uncles near the next hut.

"I tried to talk with you, to tell you how much I love you, but you refused to listen," he said.

"What are you doing?" I asked as he grabbed at my shirt. He knew I didn't like him in that way. Why was he trying to take off my clothes?

"No!" I tried to push him away and get out of the tent, but he was too strong for me. I knew my uncle was outside nearby, but if I ran outside, my uncle might kill Martin, beat me unconscious for shaming the family, force me to marry the man who had proposed earlier, or make me marry Martin. I could imagine my family telling Martin, "You've destroyed her, so now you have to take her as your wife." I shuddered.

The next thing I knew, he'd thrown me to the ground and was on top of me.

The pain was intense, and I felt as if the hut were closing in on me.

As soon as he was finished, he stood. "Get dressed," he said with no concern for what he'd just done to me. "Adam will be back soon." Then he walked out of the hut.

I felt sick and I hurt all over. But I could tell no one. *In two days, I'll be in America, and nobody there needs to know what happened to me.*

"I don't feel good," I told Adam as soon as he returned. "I should go."

"Maybe you should drink first. Are you okay?"

"No, I just want to go."

He walked me back to my hut. By the time we arrived, I really was ill; my body was sweating all over. I immediately lay on my bed.

That evening, Uncle Machok came into the hut and touched my forehead. "You *are* warm. Someone told me you've come down with malaria." He frowned for a moment, as if wondering what to do. "We don't have money to buy aspirin or Tylenol."

"That's okay." I just wanted to be by myself.

"All right," he told me. "Try to sleep. Tomorrow the community will come and pray for you and give you our send-off."

Lying in bed, I thought about the war that made us flee Sudan and all the tragedy I'd seen. It had stolen my childhood and my close family, it had broken my heart—and now this, just before I was to leave.

How can a good God let this happen? I wondered. But no answers came. And even the sky that night conspired against me. There were no stars out. The familiar stars that held my loving family had fled from me as well.

❀ ❀ ❀ ❀ ❀

The next day when I awoke, I found Uncle Machok already up and sitting with two cups of tea, one for him and one for me.

"Good morning, WunAjang." He used my nickname. "Tomorrow is the day you leave us." He lifted his teacup and encouraged me to do the same. The tea was hot and tasted sweet going down, soothing my dry throat. This was a kindness I'd rarely experienced from him, and I was grateful for it. I knew I would tuck this memory deep into my heart. I had never sat with my uncle to have tea with him before. This was a special moment.

"I want to tell you something about your father," he said. "After your mother died, your father really wanted to take you with him and your stepmother, but Kokok wouldn't allow it. She was afraid of something happening to you. So many of the girls were sold into slavery or killed or had terrible things happen to them, and she wanted to protect you from that. Your father struggled over leaving you. He had to, because he was fighting for our land

and our freedom. But it broke his heart not to have you with him."

Uncle's words touched deep in my soul. I had sometimes wondered why Baba hadn't let me go with him. Now I understood it was to keep me as safe and protected as he could. I knew Kokok had done the same for me.

Throughout the morning, people stopped by and sat next to me. No one said much. I think mostly we were just grieving the good-bye.

My cousin Monica gave me her embroidered bedsheet, which she had made. "You have this. Take it with you to America."

Later that afternoon, the women from my church came. We sang and they prayed over me. At the end of prayers, one woman, Nyandhuol Arop, gave me a wooden cross. She asked me to write her name and the date on the cross with my blue pen from the refugee school and to keep this cross to remember all the elderly women I'd beaten the drum for on their Tuesday evening worship times. Then she led the women in singing "Laare Rin ke Yecu Benydit" (Take the Name of Jesus Wherever You Go). This was one of my favorite songs, so I was happy to sing it.

"This is the song we, the women of Tuesday evening worship, greet you with," she said. "Please remember this song during your difficult time in your new land. When Satan tries to mislead you, remember and sing this song and call on Jesus' name. You are free to adopt anything in America, but don't let go of Jesus. He is your true friend and protector."

But I yearned to know why Jesus hadn't protected me the previous day. Though I was angry over what had happened to me and why, I managed to smile and thank them for their gift. The truth was, I had learned much from my church and these women—I had learned that God doesn't always keep us from experiencing trauma, but his unseen presence is with us, strengthening us.

I looked at this wonderful group who taught me about becoming a woman and, most of all, who taught me about Jesus' love, especially during the darkest times. Of everyone in the camp, I think I would miss them most.

The time finally came for us to leave, Sunday, November 5, 2000. I changed into a white T-shirt that had COCA-COLA printed on it and a long skirt. I waited for my cousins to show up, since Uncle told me they were going to give me a ride to the airstrip. But instead Luk arrived, riding a bike!

"You are not going to walk," he said proudly. "I am taking you to the airstrip. I've been saving money so I could rent this bike to take you there."

I looked at Luk, who was smiling, and mentally shrugged off my thoughts. I was happy not to be walking in the scalding heat of Kakuma.

We rode to the Kakuma airstrip, near the UN compound. There was a small plane sitting on the dusty red ground. I had to stand in a long line to get checked in by someone with a paper marking off our names as we formed the line to enter the plane. As the group grew, I felt a nervous energy among everyone, and a few whispers still hung in the air about this program being a setup to steal us away to Khartuom. But after what I'd experienced the day before, even that no longer held fear for me. I no longer cared if I did become a slave; I just didn't want to set foot in Kakuma ever again.

When everyone had arrived, a man with a clipboard called out names. Mine was called and my brother jumped up and yelled, "Here she is." He looked at me and smiled. "Go now."

The walk from the group to the small airplane wasn't far and I could hear people yelling their good-byes and shouting our names. "Don't forget about us in America!" they said. But I refused to look back.

I stepped inside the first plane I'd ever been on. I sat by the window, but still didn't look out at the crowd. The plane's propellers roared to life. Even over the noise, I could still hear the people shouting at us.

As the plane lifted off the ground, I was surprised by the stream of tears running down my face. I pushed my head against the window and looked out for the first time. A dust trail was following us, raised up from the propellers. The people were getting smaller, but I could see my friends by my brother Luk on his bike, waving at me.

God, please, when we land, if it's in Khartuom and the enemies come to take us, let them have guns, so I will run and they will shoot me, I prayed. *Lord, let them not catch me and abuse me. Let me die with the first bullet, dear God.*

It had taken me so long to get to the point where I sat on this plane. My eyes looked over this barren landscape. The camp with its densely packed mud huts and tents spread out like a large blanket over the earth. Brown dirt was everywhere. I wouldn't miss this place—a place I'd never wanted to come to, a place that my enemies had forced me to, a place where bad things had happened. I was ready to make new memories.

"Lord," I prayerfully whispered, as the earth moved farther away, "take me away on the wind to freedom or to a sweet reunion with my family in heaven." And I closed my eyes, waiting for what would happen next.

Part Four

Safe

"Give me your tired, your poor,
Your huddled masses yearning to breathe free,
The wretched refuse of your teeming shore.
Send these, the homeless, tempest-tost to me,
I lift my lamp beside the golden door!"

—Emma Lazarus,
"The New Colossus"

CHAPTER 12

Welcome to America

Less than an hour after we left Kakuma, we landed in Nairobi. Any thoughts we'd had of being tricked and shipped off to Khartoum were now fading memories. A UN person met us and escorted us as a group to a place where they gave us clothes, shoes, and a white bag with a blue circle on it. Inside the circle it said IOM, for International Organization for Immigration.

"Inside your bag is a chest X-ray, your itinerary, and your plane tickets," the UN person told us. "Hold on to this bag, don't forget it anywhere, and don't lose it. Now go change into your new clothes. You can take nothing else with you."

I put on white canvas tennis shoes, a drab gray T-shirt with the letters USRP—United States Refugee Program— across the front, and dark blue sweatpants. Because I couldn't take anything with me, I had to leave my cousin's embroidered bedsheet. That made me sad, because I knew how much work she'd put into that, and for her to give it to me was a great honor and sacrifice.

I'd brought only two other things with me—my traditional beaded waistband, which I was wearing, and the wooden cross from the ladies at my church.

No, I won't give those up, I thought, as I tucked the cross into my bag and made sure no one could see my belt hidden inside my shirt.

I looked at the group of Lost Boys and Lost Girls, as we were now called. We were a large group, although I don't know how many. We all wore the same outfit and carried the same bag. And none of us had our hair, since they'd shaved it or cut it all off.

For the next twenty-four hours I went from flight to flight—from Nairobi to Amsterdam to New York City to Chicago to Grand Rapids. At each airport, someone met me and helped me get to my next gate. In Amsterdam, the group split, which added another level of trauma, because we thought we were going to one place, but then we ended up going in different directions.

All the sights and sounds were so loud and different from anything I'd experienced, and everything was so fast paced. We had to rush to get here or there. My English was so limited, I lost more than I caught. And I was exhausted. I felt as though my brain had shut down and I couldn't concentrate or stay alert. But the food was the worst! They fed us something called broccoli, which looked like a small desert tree and tasted awful. They also fed us rich, European meals on the plane, which my body wasn't used to, having eaten refugee camp food for the past eight years. My stomach couldn't handle the taste or smell and I spent most of the flights throwing up. And the flight turbulence made me feel even worse. I was miserable, exhausted, scared, and shell-shocked all the way around. I felt like a zombie—emotionless and empty of expression. I no longer had the energy to care about what was happening to me.

As we were landing in New York, I looked out the window and recognized the Statue of Liberty, because it was on the cover of our cultural orientation book. She looked beautiful standing in the middle of the water and holding a lamp and a book. I thought about the lamp she held. The guiding star for a new hope and life. My mind went back to Kakuma Refugee Camp, my home, and how crazy and scary it was to leave that place to come to the unknown world. I was glad the person holding the lamp was a lady. My whole life, women had taken care of me, and something deep down told me to trust that my life here would be okay.

By the time we arrived in Grand Rapids—or Grand Rubbish, as I had believed it to be named—only six of the group were left together, my distant cousins on my mother's side (two boys and two girls), another boy, and me. The IOM representative told us that Bethany Christian Services was sponsoring us, so we all believed Bethany Christian Services was one family and we were all being placed together. But as we flew to Grand Rapids, they told us we were going to different towns in Michigan—and I was going to Holland.

"Wait," I said. "We are not going to Bethany Christian Services?"

The woman shook her head. "Bethany Christian Services is a settlement agency that you are coming through. You have your own family to go with."

So we really are all being separated, I thought. Tears sprang to my eyes as I wondered if I'd ever see my cousins or the others again.

We landed late in the evening. As I walked off the plane and into the waiting area, I blinked at the bright lights of the airport, but also at the sea of white people. At the refugee camp, we saw one or two every once in a while, and on the trip from Kakuma, we saw them blended in with other races—but *every* face in this entire airport was white! And they were all staring at us and smiling. Television crews and people with cameras were everywhere.

God, I don't care what color my family is, just please let them know Jesus, I prayed silently. At least if they knew Jesus, we'd have something in common.

I was assigned a social worker who led me to my new family. Three people—all pasty white and very young looking—stood smiling and waiting to greet me. They had kind eyes. The man introduced himself as Lennis Baggech, but I couldn't quite get his name. Another lady, whom I assumed was the mom, said her name, Heather, but I couldn't remember it. When their daughter introduced herself, I was surprised that she had a British accent. Her name was Rachel. I'd heard of that name before, because it was a biblical name and I had friends in Kakuma named Rachel.

Rachel hugged me and held my hand. Then the man, my foster father, said, *"Habari yako?"* That meant "How are you?" in Swahili. My eyes lit up and I said in Swahili, *"Wewe ni Dinka nzuri?"* ("You are a good Dinka?") He laughed and said something broken. His Swahili was as bad as my English, but I loved that he'd made that gesture.

Rachel wrapped her arm around my waist, and we walked outside to their car. As soon as the cold November air slapped my face, I stopped, shocked. I'd never felt wind so cold before.

We got into the car and Lennis turned on the heat. Rachel put me in the front, next to Lennis, because I was still feeling sick. She sat in the back with my new mother, Heather.

As we drove away I tried to take in the surroundings, but they were difficult to see since it was dark. But one thing I did see—all the trees were dead. Nothing was green, none of the trees had any leaves on them. And there were so many cars on big roads, all zooming around. I couldn't understand how they avoided hitting one another.

What kind of place is this? I wondered.

There is a Dinka saying that goes like this: "First word, said the crocodile." It means the first word that comes out of somebody's mouth is the true representation of their thoughts, values, and beliefs about themselves or you, so it is important always to be careful about that first word. I chose my word carefully.

"Church?" I said.

It took them a moment to understand what I was asking, but then Lennis said, "Yes! Yes, we go to church."

Those were the most beautiful English words I'd ever heard. I knew my life going forward was going to be difficult—a new culture, a new people, a new language—but we both knew Jesus, and I knew then I was going to be okay.

We pulled up to my new home and my foster mother got out and hugged me and then walked toward a car. She was leaving? I didn't understand what was going on until through my broken understanding of English I finally realized that woman wasn't my mother! She was a friend of my new family's who had come along for support. I looked at the woman whom I thought to be my sister but who was actually my foster mother. She looked so young! She told me she was twenty-eight, and I was their first child. I was too tired and confused to figure it all out, so I just nodded and followed them into the most beautiful house I'd ever been in.

As soon as I stepped through the door, a big, black dog jumped out at us. She barked and wagged her tail. I couldn't believe they had a dog in the house, since we never had animals in our huts. But also this dog was fat, unlike the skinny dogs in Sudan. Lennis knelt down, laughed, and began to kiss it. I'd never seen anybody do that with an animal either.

"Come in, Rebecca," Rachel said. "Let me show you around."

As we walked into room after room, I could hardly take it all in. They slept and cooked in the same house. They even had a bathroom inside the house—and it wasn't a pit latrine; they pushed on a handle and water flushed everything away!

She showed me how to get water. It was like magic. I wouldn't have to pump to get it. I just lifted a knob and out it came. And I could make it cold or hot!

Then she opened a door and flipped a switch on the wall. Immediately light flooded the room, making me squint. "This is your room," she said. "And that is your bed." She nodded toward what looked like a fluffy mat on short stilts. I looked back and forth between the bed and her.

Where is my mat to sleep on? I wondered.

As if reading my mind, Rachel smiled and walked to the bed. "You sleep here. These are covers to keep you warm," she said, pulling them back. "This is your pillow. You'll put your head on it. Then you put your body in between these sheets."

She handed me some clothes and told me I could sleep in them. She called them "pajamas." They were pretty and soft.

When she left, I noticed teddy bears on the bed. *What are these animal-like creatures doing here?* I thought as I threw them all on the floor. *They have a dog in the house and now these creatures?* I didn't understand any of this.

I tucked my body into the bed, just as she'd shown me. The bed was soft, but it felt weird to sleep on something raised above the ground. Though I had a window in my room, it was across from my bed. Even when I tried to look out, I saw no stars, only a dark, bleak night.

"God, thank you for bringing me here, but I'm not sure how I'm going to do," I prayed. "Protect me and help me adapt to my new home. And, Lord, please be with my family and friends back in Kakuma."

Then I wrapped the sheets around my head, as I'd done for eight years to keep the sand out of my face and ears and to protect me from any invaders, and fell asleep.

* * * * *

I didn't sleep well. It was too quiet and dark. When I awoke the next morning, there was no sun outside, no noise of roosters, chickens, or people talking like in our Kakuma Refugee Camp.

Where am I? I wondered, feeling confused and out of sorts. *Why is it so quiet and dark?* Then I realized I'd spent my first night at my new home in the United States.

I opened the door of my room, but right outside the door were stairs! How had I not noticed them the night before?

What if I fall? I thought. *Why do these people put stairs in the house?* Our houses in the refugee camp were just one big space and everybody slept there. Then it hit me—I had just spent a night by myself for the first time in my fifteen years of life. In the village, I shared a mat with Kokok, and at Kakuma I shared one with my girl cousins. My uncle and his wife didn't sleep far from us. We could hear their breathing and they could hear ours.

I grabbed onto the railing attached to the wall and made my way down the steps, then wandered through the house until I found the kitchen, where my foster parents were.

"Good morning, Rebecca," my foster father said, smiling. "I made you some food, if you'd like." Instinctively I touched my stomach. If this food was anything like what I'd eaten on the planes, I wasn't interested.

He told me to sit at their table and he put a bowl of steaming porridge in front of me. Hesitantly, I took a few bites. It tasted good, like what I was used to.

"Would you like *mandazi*?" he asked.

They have mandazi here? I thought and got excited. He took me to the place called Donutville, where they sold mandazi. It was sweeter than what I was used to, but at least it was like being back home.

I still couldn't get used to how dead everything was, though. I asked them what happened to all the trees, and they told me the leaves would come back on the trees in the spring. I thought they were crazy—what kind of tree died for a season and then got new leaves again? But they said that happened every year. Deep down I didn't believe them. When I last saw trees looking that dead, our village was attacked and set on fire. I went outside to examine the trees to see if the branches were charred, but only the leaves were missing. I was confused.

A couple days later, I received an even bigger shock. My dad woke me one morning and told me to look outside. I rubbed my eyes and went to the window. I had to blink several times. Big, white things were falling from the sky. Millions of them! They were landing everywhere and covering the ground.

I swallowed hard, terror filling me. *It's the end of the world!*

I thought. *Jesus is coming. Why would he bring me to the other side of the world, away from my family and friends, if he was going to come days after I got here?*

I looked at Lennis, confused why he wasn't as scared as I was. But he was laughing and smiling. "This is snow! You're going to see a lot of it now that you live in Michigan."

This new place was crazy.

My foster parents tried to speak in Swahili as much as they could, which I appreciated, since learning English and speaking it full-time is so different. They were difficult to understand, though. My American dad had a strange accent. My mother did too, but she was British, so I was able to understand her English a bit better, since a lot of British aid workers were in the refugee camp. When I called her Mom, she asked me to call her "Mum" instead, since that was her British/Scottish upbringing.

For the next week or so, we took life slowly. My foster parents stayed close to me, doing their best to make me feel as comfortable as possible. Every Sunday they drove me to Hudsonville, where my cousins were living with their foster families, so we could go to church together. And they did their best to help me stay in contact with the refugees who had come from Sudan. They were very compassionate toward me, as if they understood that I felt traumatized by everything I'd gone through. I learned both Lennis and Rachel had spent time working in Africa several years before, so they knew about the land I came from, and that helped comfort me too.

My dad always tried to make me laugh and put me at

ease. He loved to say, "Watch this, Rebecca, it's magic!" Then he'd jump in front of the garage door and it would open!

One time he took me to a Meijer store. I'd never seen such a big marketplace. We only had small shops back in Kenya. As we were approaching the door, I didn't see any gates, only glass, and Dad was walking straight toward it.

Maybe he wants to look at it or use it as a mirror, I thought. I kept following him and he said, "Rebecca, watch this. I'm going to open the door without using my hands." And sure enough, just as we got to the glass, he waved his arms and it opened! I jumped back. *What is happening?* Did my eyes just see a glass opening but no broken glass on the floor?

It was scary and cool at the same time. We went from aisle to aisle—with more food than I'd ever seen in my life. I also noticed there were a lot of people who looked like my dad. I became scared that I was going to lose him, because this place was so big and the people all looked the same. "Dad, what if I lose you in here?" I said. "I won't find you and won't know how because there are so many white people."

He nodded. "Look closely at my ears." He pointed at one of them, where I saw a small cut. "That's how you will know it's me. But I promise I'll always be around you. If something happens and you do lose me, I will look for *you.* Okay?"

I was glad he said that, because how was I going to look at all the white people's ears in this market?

We filled the shopping cart and went to a line to wait to

pay. It reminded me of the ration line at Kakuma, but there no one was given a choice over what they put in their cart.

Everything was so different and overwhelming. They cooked in boxes called microwaves, kept milk cold in refrigerators, and didn't have to grind corn flour every day to make paste. They could simply open a can and food would pour out, ready to heat and eat. The weather was dismal and cold. Everybody spoke English too quickly. And I didn't see hardly anybody else who looked like me.

But the nights were the hardest. Every night I covered my head tightly in my sheets to protect myself, but still I dreamed of all kinds of attacks. Men wanted to chop off my head or put bullets in me. I would scream and wake up to Mum's hands on my forehead comforting me. She would pray with me until my breathing returned to normal, my dreams had passed, and I felt safe again. She told me everything was okay, that they were here, and she stayed with me until I fell back asleep. But still I struggled. My head told me I was safe in the United States, but my dreams kept taking me back to the terrors of my past.

When I felt especially overwhelmed, I kept everything to myself and pretended that I wasn't hurting or thinking about my friends and family I'd left in the refugee camp. I was afraid if I talked all the time about my relatives back home or at the refugee camp, my foster family might get mad at me and not love me. I knew very well that feeling of not being accepted, and I didn't want that feeling here in America. After all, I was an orphan, and if God gave me a second chance to have a family, I should hold on tight.

But I experienced good things too. One day as Mum and I were sitting together, she grunted a little, then she smiled brightly. "I'm five months pregnant. The baby just moved. Here," she said and put my hand on her belly. I felt something moving inside! My aunts and cousins back at Kakuma had never let me do this thing. They never even mentioned about the baby moving. They just kept up with their work. But this was a wonder!

Dad came over to us. "Rebecca, we are going to have a baby!" He put his head on her belly for a minute and then he kissed her. They were kind and compassionate parents, and I knew God had placed me with them for a purpose.

Once I felt a bit more acclimated, my parents walked me to my new school, Holland Christian. The school principal placed me in ninth grade, but I didn't attend regular classes like the other students. Instead, I sat with some English as a Second Language (ESL) teachers and they read magazines to me, since my English was so poor. By the end of each day my head was spinning, and I worried I would never be able to understand it all.

One of my ESL teachers found a book by a former refugee from Ethiopia who had resettled in Chicago and then attended Harvard. My teacher read me his stories, which I could relate to and which helped me understand better. That was the turning point for me. Unlike other stories they read to me, I could see myself in this one. This man, this refugee, had become somebody. *Wow!* I thought.

The food was still terrible and I still struggled to comprehend the language, but slowly I began to adjust to my new life and believe that I could succeed here. One day about a month after I'd been in America, Mum announced that I was getting a new sister and how exciting that was going to be.

"You know what your baby is going to be?" I asked, wondering how anybody could know such a thing before the baby was born.

"No," she said and laughed. "We're getting another refugee from Sudan. She is coming soon and her name is Teresa."

"That sounds good," I said, glad to have somebody who would understand my culture and whom I could speak my language with.

The day she arrived, we picked her up from the airport and I recognized her immediately. I'd gone to school with her at the Kakuma girl's boarding school. And there was one very big problem with her: She was Nuer, the Dinka's rival tribe. Worse, though: Hers was the tribe that had forced my family to flee our village.

CHAPTER 13

A New Way of Life

Dad and Mum put Teresa Nyaruach Wien in the same room with me. After all, we were from the same country, so they believed everything would be great. What many people failed to understand was that Sudan had more than sixty-five different tribes—and not all of them got along.

At first I was happy to have Teresa there with us, as she was a link to my homeland. Plus, she was fun to be around. We both loved to dance, and she was easy to talk to. We braided each other's hair as it began to grow, and we attended the same ESL class and gym class. We also gossiped about the things we didn't understand about American culture, such as people kissing in public and children disagreeing with their parents and voicing their beliefs.

We especially loved watching *The Lion King*. The way Africa was portrayed comforted us and made us laugh. We sang the songs along with the characters and cried every time Simba's father died. We watched it together over and over. We also enjoyed watching *Veggie Tales*. Although we were teenagers, the children's shows helped as we tried to learn English. My favorite *Veggie Tales* video was *Madame*

Blueberry. She would cry and sing, "I am so blue, blue, and I don't know what to do."

Even though Teresa was from my homeland, I still missed my family. And when I felt particularly overwhelmed because we were often the only black people among all the whites in Holland, I would think of Madame Blueberry and secretly sing to myself, "I am so black, black, and I don't know what to do."

Though Teresa also spoke little English, and the Dinka language and the Nuer language are different, we mixed Dinka, Nuer, Swahili, and broken English to form our own way of communicating. We understood enough of each other that we were able to get along. And we did. For a couple months.

But we came from the Dinka and Nuer who had wounded each other. Those hostilities ran deep and were ingrained in our thoughts toward each other. Being young, we didn't know better.

Tensions started with stupid arguments over which tribe was better and stronger. I knew they came from a place of fear, I knew I shouldn't have let our comments bother me, but at times I couldn't let it go. We were in the new land of freedom and a fresh start, but our wounds from the past kept us hostage. Too often we took it out on each other.

But soon I faced something else from my past that held me hostage, forcing me to ignore our hostilities toward each other. By February I still had no period. Every time I raised my concern to Mum, she reassured me, saying it was the stress and trauma I'd endured or the change in my diet. "Sometimes young women won't regain their period for six months," she said. "It's not a big deal." But when it still didn't come, Mum suggested I see a doctor.

"Let's put her on a hormone injection to induce her period," the doctor said. "We should do a pregnancy test first, though, just to be sure."

"She had a test done the day before she came to the US," Mum said. "That came up negative. And she's been with us ever since."

The doctor nodded and furrowed his brow. "Well, let's check anyway."

After we left the doctor's office, Mum stopped off at the drugstore and bought a pregnancy test. She explained that I would have to pee on a stick. Teresa and I laughed at that. So many of these American ways made no sense and seemed crazy to me.

"You're probably pregnant," Teresa told me when I got home.

"What? No, I couldn't be." But I felt uneasy about her comment, because she seemed more insightful than me.

"Well, did you do anything before you left Kakuma?"

I told her about what had happened with Martin, but I couldn't believe that would be the reason for me not to have a period.

She nodded and frowned. "Let me do it for you."

I understood what she was saying. She was willing to help me, because we both knew if I was pregnant, our parents might become angry, believing I'd lied to them. They might want to send me back to Kakuma. That would be the death of me for certain. My family would be shamed and would probably force me to marry Martin. No, I couldn't let that happen.

I looked at Teresa. We might not always get along, but I was grateful she was willing to do this for me.

So with a "negative" pregnancy test outcome, the doctor gave me the hormone injection. For five days, I waited. When my period still didn't arrive, the doctor suggested I have an ultrasound.

"This is the coolest thing! It'll be easy," Mum explained. She must have sensed how terrified I was. "The technician puts something on your belly, and you can see inside all your organs. We could see my baby in there when they did it for me." She pointed to her expanded stomach. "It's not scary at all."

I said okay, even though I still wasn't sure about it. Teresa was intrigued too and wanted to go, so we made it into a family trip. Everyone joked about how they were going to get to see my kidneys.

The day came for my ultrasound, and Mum, Dad, Teresa, and I were all happy and laughing. A pleasant-looking woman in a white coat came in. She lifted my shirt and moved my beaded waistband out of the way, then she squirted a cool, clear, jellylike substance onto my stomach and ran a wand over it. She looked at the screen and smiled. I could see the screen too, but I wasn't sure what I was supposed to see. I'd never learned what kidneys looked like, so everything appeared blurry.

Dad and Teresa kept saying, "Wow!"

The woman moved the wand around a couple of times, staring at the screen. Then she looked at Mum, who was also watching the screen. She took my mum's arm and whispered, "Is this why you're here?"

Mum whispered something back, which I couldn't catch. The next thing I knew, Mum left my side and told Dad and Teresa to go outside with her. Teresa became indignant, asking why she had to leave just as the fun part was starting.

"Come on, Teresa, let's go," Dad told her and led her to the hallway, followed by the technician.

I wished someone would have told me what was going on and why they all left. *Is there something wrong with my kidneys?* I wondered.

Mum soon came back in alone. She sat next to the bed, took my hand, and tried to look in my eyes, but I looked away. A bad feeling washed over me, as though I knew she was going to tell me I had something terribly wrong with my body.

"Rebecca," she said calmly, "do you know you're pregnant?"

I swallowed hard but still wouldn't look at her. *A baby?* I thought. *How can I have a baby?* And then another thought hit me. *Teresa was right.* I felt my eyes fill with tears.

"It's okay. Do you want to tell me the story?"

Yeah, something happened in the refugee camp, I thought, but I couldn't tell her that. Could I trust her? Would she even believe me? Would I bring shame to this family?

"I know you were engaged. Is it that man?"

It wasn't him, but I didn't want to talk about what had really happened. It was too horrible. Instead I nodded slowly. "Uh-huh," I said, feeling overwhelmed and trying to process everything.

She squeezed my hand lightly. "It's okay. We'll get through this together. Dad and I love you, Becca."

How is this possible? I wondered. I thought when people got pregnant, they had to be married and live with their husband for a while, and then they could become pregnant. How could I be pregnant? I didn't even know *how* to get pregnant!

I wished my science teacher back at the refugee school had taught us about that. I remembered the one time when the teacher showed pictures of women's private parts. Some of the boys turned around and looked at us girls and chuckled. I was so embarrassed that I looked at the ground until the lesson was over. I didn't hear anything the teacher said.

The more I thought about it, the more I convinced myself that I wasn't pregnant. *Maybe something went wrong and they just don't know. Maybe they just* think *I'm pregnant.*

Nobody spoke on the drive home, for which I was grateful. I was in a daze, going through the motions of walking from the car to the house. As soon as we got home, I fell on the couch, curled into a tight ball, and lay there letting the tears stream from my eyes. Mum sat beside me and rubbed my back. She even made me tea, which I normally loved drinking, but nothing made me want to uncurl.

"Rebecca," she said softly, lifting my arm to help me up. "Let's go upstairs."

She and I made it to the bottom of the steps when I stopped. I reached under my shirt and felt for the intricately beaded traditional waistband I wore, which consisted of thousands of tiny brightly colored beads. I'd noticed recently it was fitting more snuggly; now I understood why.

I grabbed it, suddenly aware there would be no room for it with my swelling stomach, and I jerked it free. As the beads broke loose, they fell to the floor, bouncing and rolling into corners. I dropped the rest of the band, left it in a pile on the floor, and went to my room.

I lay on my bed and looked up at the ceiling, wondering what this now meant for me. I'd have to quit school and give up all the things I'd dreamed of for my life. I wanted to be educated, to go to college and help people. How could I do any of those things? And how could I tell my Sudanese community? They'd been my lifeline to my family back in Africa, but they would want to pressure me into getting married. And anyway, how could I be a mother? I didn't know how to be a mother! I'd lost mine when I was so young I could barely remember her. And then I'd lost Kokok.

God, what is happening?

Hot, salty tears flowed down my cheeks and onto my pillow, and soon sobs came, hard and fast, leaving me breathless.

The door quietly opened. My dad entered the room and sat on the edge of the bed. "Becca, it's going to be all right," he said. "Your mum and I are here for you." He scooped me into his arms, and I felt safe. He stayed with me almost the entire night as I cried until I had nothing left in me.

The next day I called one of my cousins in Hudsonville and told her the news. I knew she would tell the rest of our Sudanese community in Michigan, but I also knew they were going to find out at some point anyway. She was compassionate as she listened, then suggested that I get married. "Why not marry the baby's father? If he likes you and will care for your baby, what is the harm?"

"The harm is that I don't want to marry someone I don't love or respect," I told her. "Besides, I'm only sixteen. That may be a marriageable age back in Sudan, but it certainly isn't here in America. I want to finish my education. That's why I came here."

She listened and said she understood.

Now I knew I needed to tell my foster parents the truth. Though I was scared, one evening after supper when we were alone, I said, "Mum, Dad, I need to tell you something important. I told you I got pregnant from the man I was engaged to marry, but that isn't the truth." I confessed everything that had happened to me. If they no longer loved me, or forced me from their family, then so be it. I didn't want to live a lie.

They both listened quietly, their eyes filled with compassion, which gave me the strength to tell them everything.

"You know, Rebecca, after I graduated from college,

I had a girlfriend," Dad told me after I finished talking. "She had one more year in school. By that time I'd moved away, so we were dating long-distance. But I noticed after the school year started, she became cold and distant. I couldn't understand what had happened to make her that way. Then a couple months later, she called and told me that when she got back to school in September, she'd gone jogging early one morning in a cemetery and a man chased her and raped her. She got pregnant. She hadn't told her parents. She hadn't reported it to the police. Nobody. She was an innocent victim. Just as *you* are an innocent victim."

I looked into my father's eyes and saw tears there. His comforting words and actions meant so much to me. He didn't blame me for what had happened. He knew it wasn't my fault.

"There's something else," I said. I told them that my Sudanese community might pressure me to quit school and get married. My parents would often drive me to Grand Rapids to visit the other Lost Boys and Lost Girls in the area, as well as other people from my tribe. It didn't matter that we all now lived in the United States with a different culture; they were committed to living by the Dinka code, which had strict beliefs about women and their place in the community. I was pregnant—it didn't matter how I got that way—so to their way of thinking, as long as the man who gave me the baby wanted to marry me, that was fine and I should agree to it. Because they didn't know the whole story, they wouldn't understand my refusal.

"Is that what you want?" Mum asked.

"No. I know I'll have to raise this child on my own, but I'd rather do that than marry someone I don't love or respect who says he loves me but doesn't respect me."

"That won't be an option either," Mum said. "We'll help you raise this child so you can continue your education. You don't have to marry anybody or raise the baby on your own. You aren't alone in this, Rebecca."

I couldn't believe what Mum and Dad were offering. "But you're going to have your own baby. How can you handle mine too?"

"We'll manage. God will help us," Mum said. "It's going to be okay."

I knew right then I could trust them, that they wouldn't leave me or force me to marry someone against my will. Although I was still terrified to have a baby, I knew I wouldn't have to face it alone. And for the first time since I could remember, I stopped wrapping my head in the sheets when I went to bed at night. I no longer feared that someone would come and grab me in the darkness. And my nightmares slowly stopped tormenting me as well.

Mum gave birth to Aidan in March 2001. Teresa and I both loved holding and cuddling him. And for the first time in my pregnancy, I began to see how precious having a baby could be. I knew I didn't want to give up my child to adoption, but I also knew at sixteen years old I wasn't ready to become a full-time mother. Fortunately, Mum prepared me by showing me how to change a diaper and feed Aidan when he cried.

I finished my first school year in May. And in June

a team of teachers from Holland Christian came to our house and converted our basement into bedrooms so we'd have space for two babies and two teenagers. Our family was suddenly growing fast.

By July 19, my own time came to give birth. The labor was intense and long. With everything I'd been through, I'd still never experienced pain as terrible as I did giving birth. Through the long hours of waiting and aching, I found myself thinking about my own mother. She had been in labor when the first attack on our village came. I couldn't imagine what she must have gone through, trying to have a baby and run for her life in the midst of so much terror.

I looked around the sterile room with its calm music playing and people smiling and encouraging me. So different from my mother's experience. I missed my mother. I missed Kokok. I knew they would have loved seeing and holding my new baby.

Finally, after twenty hours of labor, on the evening of July 20, 2001, my little girl entered the world—six pounds, nine ounces, and twenty-one inches long. She was a long baby—a true Dinka, a Nilotic Nubian princess. I named her Achol after my mother, whose name means "the one who replaces your sorrow with joy." My foster parents added the name Lauren, and we gave her their last name, Baggech. We call her Cholie.

Growing up, I was so afraid of thunder. The sound rolling through the swamplands sank my heart every time—even though I loved everything else that came with the rain: the fresh smells, the lightning, and finally the rainbow. Over time, my fear of rain disappeared as I waited for the promise of the rainbow. I couldn't believe how a frightening event could turn so beautiful at the end. When the rain stopped, I'd quickly jump outside to look for the rainbow's different colors in the sky. *How does God do that?* I'd often wonder, admiring such beauty.

When things got dark with the news that at sixteen, I was going to have a baby from a man I would never marry, I was filled with fears. Though I knew I had loving support from my foster parents, I still felt lost.

Then came the rainbow of my life—Cholie. Holding her at the hospital for the first time after such a long labor, I remembered the Dinka saying: "It is what you have borne or that of the womb that redeems you." For the first time it made sense to me. Cholie cleansed me of all the hurt and betrayal I felt. When I looked at her beautiful face, the overwhelming love I had for her freed me to finally love myself. And slowly the chains around my heart were breaking. All the anger, hatred, pain, even self-hatred began to break loose. Cholie made it possible for me to begin to forgive.

For the next two months, before school started, I spent all my time with my new daughter, breastfeeding her and learning how to be a mom. Cholie was a good baby. She didn't cry much and smiled easily. I loved holding her, playing with her, and taking care of her. And she seemed to love being close to me.

When Cholie was six weeks old, Mum and I took the

babies to Scotland, where she is originally from. She wanted her Scottish family to meet us. The trip opened my eyes to how much my mum and I had in common. Although she wasn't a refugee or had to flee, she *had* chosen to give up the familiar things of her family and country to form a new life and new bonds in America, just as I had. My time spent with her Scottish family helped me see that family doesn't have to be blood or sharing the same accent. Family is made by choosing to love one another.

When we returned from Scotland, school was about to start and it was time to get my mind back on my studies. Now I wasn't just studying to make something of myself; I wanted to become something so my daughter could have a good role model and learn about the importance of education. I wanted her to grow up learning that God created her for a purpose and that she could one day fulfill the desires of her heart and the dreams God had for her. That meant I must do the same—even though I hated not being with her all day every day.

Mum and Dad stepped in and willingly took over as Cholie's parents so I could attend school, and I became more like a big sister. It allowed me to still be with my daughter, but not have the pressure of balancing school work with full-time parenting. It was definitely a sacrifice, but I am grateful they offered me such a precious gift.

🍁 🍁 🍁 🍁 🍁

Though Cholie brought peace and joy in my life, I still struggled to keep up with everything that was going on around me—a baby, life in a new world and culture, my struggles with school and learning English, pressure from the Sudanese community, and continued tensions with Teresa.

My relationship with Teresa hit a wall on September 11, 2001, when fear was in the air. The world's most powerful country had just been attacked, sending Teresa and me mentally back to revisit our Sudanese wars and tragedies. The terrorist attack terrified everyone, especially Teresa and me, because we heard the word *jihad* against the United States and it took us back to the fear of the war and the trauma of what we'd experienced. After school we started saying mean things about each other's tribes.

That was all it took. Months of pent-up hostility and anger boiled over, and I slapped her face. The fight began. She bit my arm, drawing blood, and we were both pulling each other's hair and hitting and kicking each other all the way up the driveway and up the cement stairs at the side of our house. I grabbed her head and shoved it hard against the cement.

"Girls! Stop it! Stop it right now!" Mum was holding both the babies and yelling at us from an open window. Neither of us listened. It was as if a dam broke and we were taking out on each other years of frustration and anger over what we'd endured.

Soon the back door opened and Mum was in between us trying to get us to break it up, but still we continued.

"Teresa, knock it off. Rebecca, stop!" she said. "I'm going to count to ten, and if you don't quit this, I'm calling the police."

I didn't care. I'd had enough of being bullied my whole life. Her people had been the reason everyone I loved in my family was dead, why I had no beautiful village to live in. Why I was an orphan. I wanted to make her pay.

By the time the police arrived, Teresa and I were both spent and the pain was beginning to throb.

"No more fighting," a police officer told us. "Otherwise, we'll take you to juvenile detention."

For the next several weeks Teresa and I didn't speak to each other. My Dinka community wanted me to leave the house and couldn't understand why Mum and Dad made us live together. Teresa begged to be placed with a different family, but our parents explained that we were family and they weren't going to budge. We would need to learn to get along, because that's what family does.

By then I'd started to calm down. I began to feel badly about how I'd reacted. Especially every time I saw her swollen face. It looked terrible—and I'd done that to her. That wasn't the kind of person I wanted to be. Somehow deep inside I began to realize that Teresa was just as wounded by the war as I was. She'd had terrible things happen to her, just as I had. And neither of us knew how to handle the trauma well. We were kids who learned while growing up that our tribes should be hostile toward each other. We had an ingrained fear of each other that wanted to steal something beautiful we had—our love for each other and friendship. That is what evil does: It keeps us hostage and covers our eyes to a renewal of life.

Slowly we began to mend our relationship, being kinder

to each other. We talked about how we wanted to bring peace between our tribes one day and how we could work to show our love and respect for each other. I think having separate bedrooms definitely helped. It also helped that I'd begun to make friends at school.

For months I'd been separated from the rest of my classmates, because I was so unsure of myself with English. Eventually, though, my school counselor assigned me to classes away from the ESL classroom. The first class was choir, which was good because I liked to sing. And the teacher said it would help me learn English.

Then the teachers told me I was going to different classes—PE and English and math. The first day I was set to switch classes, I didn't understand that when a bell rang, everyone grabbed their books and raced into the hallways. I thought we were being attacked. At my school at the refugee camp and even at the Kenyan school I attended for a semester, when the bell rang the teachers moved from class to class, not the students.

So when the bell rang and everybody left the room, I wasn't sure what was going on. The teacher told me I had to go to my next class. But as soon as I walked into the hallway, I plastered myself against a wall. People were heading in every direction, opening their lockers, racing around. I stood and watched everyone, because I didn't know what to do.

"Do you know where you're going?" a teacher asked me.

"No," I said. "Why is everybody rushing? Is it an attack?"

"No, they're going to whatever class they have next. Let me see your schedule." She looked it over. "I'll walk you there, okay?"

It took me a long time to get used to all the rushing around and making each class before the bell rang.

As I became more comfortable with the classes, I met new people. It didn't matter to them that I barely understood what they were saying; they were patient with me and gave me confidence to learn English. I found that I was in a place where I could make mistakes and not be laughed at. I was free to fail and get up again, and that was what I did. I knew I would never speak or write English like a native, but my friends didn't seem to care. They accepted me just as I was.

Though I still missed the familiar place of Kakuma with my family and my tribe, this place was finally becoming home. I had a new family, new friends. I was pursuing my dreams. And most of all, I was safe.

Part Five

Promise

Peace will bless us once more with hearing the happy giggling of children and the enchanting ululations of women who are excited in happiness for one reason or another . . .

From here on, Sudan for the first time will be a country voluntarily united in justice, honor, and dignity for all its citizens regardless of their race, regardless of their religion, regardless of their gender.

> —John Garang, at the signing
> ceremony of the South Sudan
> peace deal

CHAPTER 14

Pursuit of a Calling

Although I struggled through four years of high school, working hard to understand English, I graduated. I had done it. The boys at Kakuma's refugee school had taunted that I would never make it past the eighth grade, no matter how smart I was. I proved them wrong!

From the time I wrote my first English alphabet on the sand of Kakuma Refugee Camp, my dream was that someday I would graduate from eighth grade and know how to read labels on medicine bottles for my children. I would also be able to communicate with others who didn't speak my Dinka language. That was my dream, as simple as it was, and I knew it would be possible if I got the opportunity to go to school and study hard. Many of my family at Kakuma knew of my dreams, and when they learned I was going to the United States, they encouraged me to pursue my schoolwork. "Education is your mother and father," they told me. "You are an orphan, and if you are educated, the knowledge will be your missing parents and relatives."

I had achieved—I had exceeded—those dreams, and now I wanted more.

I applied to and was accepted at Calvin College, a small Christian liberal arts school in Grand Rapids, not far from Holland. That gave me independence, but also kept me close enough to home that I could see Cholie and my family at least once a week. Calvin had appealed to me the first time I visited, because the weekend I went there happened to be an international regalia, in which students from all over the world gave dancing performances. I watched, amazed, and was the most comfortable I'd felt in a school setting. I knew it was the place for me.

In September 2004, I moved into the dorms on campus excited and nervous, but ready to begin.

I met my roommate, Clara, for the first time. She was a mix of five ethnicities and she grew up in Guinea, West Africa, because her parents were missionaries there. She had light skin, smelled of sweet perfume, and was dainty. I wasn't sure we would get along, because I was so different. But that afternoon it rained, and both of us ran to the dorm window, threw it open, and stuck our heads out to smell the rain. Those who live in Africa understand that fresh smell of rain hitting dry earth. I knew right then that God had placed us together. I'd found a sister.

That calmed my nerves about making a friend while I was there, but I worried about the studying part. Everyone said college was more difficult than high school, and I could only imagine what my classes were going to be like. Even though I'd worked hard, my reading was still at about a fourth-grade level.

During the first week, the professor of my literacy and

philosophy class handed me a sixty-page book with the assignment to read it and write a short report on it.

Sixty pages! I thought in a panic. *I've never even finished thirty pages. How am I supposed to do this in two weeks?*

Even worse, each page was filled with words I couldn't understand. I felt myself sink deep into sadness.

I have no idea what this book is saying! I thought, so I turned it upside down.

"What are you doing?" Clara asked.

"Maybe I'll understand it this way." I didn't. My eyes started to water and my head pounded. At least in high school, we read short stories or magazine articles. But this book was thick, and the writing was tiny, with no pictures.

I put the book down on my bed and picked up my cell phone. After a couple rings, Mum's sweet voice answered. "Becca, it's good to hear from you. How are you doing?"

"Terrible!" I burst out. "Can you come get me? I don't think I can do college. It's too much. I can't even understand what I'm reading. And the book is so big—how am I going to get through it? And we're supposed to finish it in a week and write a book report on it!"

"I know it's hard, but just keep working at it. Even if you read one line and go to the next one. Just keep pushing. You can do this."

I hung up and sighed heavily. This was what I wanted, but I didn't think it would come so hard for me. I rubbed my eyes and picked up the book again. "Okay, I can do this. Just read one line. Don't pay attention to anything else. Just one line."

I read that line slowly and contemplated what it said. Once I was satisfied that I grasped at least some of its meaning, I moved on to the next line. I refused to allow myself to be overwhelmed by the length of the book. "Just one line, just one line," I told myself over and over.

Clara suggested I go to the learning center. "People will help you," she said.

I took her advice and connected with one of the student mentors. She looked at the book and said, "Okay. This book has this many chapters, and the author is talking about this. So when you read, you need to know these are the main things."

She made it much simpler to understand! She also told me that when I wrote my report, she'd edit it for me and help me understand where I was making mistakes. The learning center became my lifesaver.

For the next four years I kept my head down in my studies, working hard, making friends, and polishing my English. At first I thought I'd major in sociology, because I wanted to better understand people groups, because of everything I'd gone through in my life. But during my sophomore year, I took an international studies class and a whole new world opened to me! I realized that if I wanted to make a difference in my home country and help people around the world understand the devastation war plays on innocent people, this was the major that would help me do that. So I switched to an international development studies major and a social work minor. I wasn't sure what I was going to do with it, but I knew God had led me to this place and he would open doors for me.

It was important to me to make English-speaking friends, because I wanted to assimilate into my new home's culture. While I continued to spend time with my Sudanese community, I limited my exposure to them, mostly because I needed to focus on my life and studies. I needed to learn about myself and my calling in this great world. To me these things had to be accomplished outside of strict rules, mind-sets, or one worldview.

Not that I wanted to completely rid myself of my people. That wasn't it at all. I love my Sudanese community. Within it incredible and wonderful things happen—they are tight-knit and look out for one another; they are respectful and kind to visitors; they understand the importance of elders and their honored place in society. I simply wanted to expand my horizons and who I was. I believed that if God brought me to this country and gave me all these opportunities, then I had a responsibility to fulfill the purpose he had given me. And I believed part of that was to become my own person, an independent woman. And to become an American citizen.

In 2006, I became an American citizen with an official ceremony and swearing in. My friends Karen, Megan, Lara, and Jacqueline even baked a cake and decorated it red, white, and blue so we could celebrate. It felt wonderful to belong and know I was safe.

By the second semester of my sophomore year in 2006,

I finally began to feel free and more sure of myself, so when an opportunity arose to study for a semester abroad in Chiang Mai, Thailand, at the International Sustainable Development Studies Institute, I took it. I figured it would be perfect for my international development studies degree. While I was there, I visited a Burmese refugee camp, which further cemented my decision to help others. I knew I wanted to help people who had been oppressed or discriminated against find freedom.

I wanted us to be able to celebrate our differences—something I saw up close and personal when, while at Calvin, I took a part-time job working at a lingerie store. One day a woman entered the shop with her four-year-old son. I approached them and asked if I could help her find anything. The little boy looked at me with widened eyes and yelled, "Mom! Look at the big talking chocolate!"

The woman grabbed her son and fled the store without so much as a word to me. My coworkers and supervisor all apologized for what had happened, although it wasn't their fault.

"I feel sorry for her, not for me," I told them. "I'm not offended by what that little boy said. Children are the most honest people in the world. Maybe that boy had never seen anybody as dark as I am. When I first saw white people, I thought they didn't have skin and that their eyes looked like cat eyes!"

Two weeks later the woman reentered the store, this time without her son. She made a beeline for me and said, "I'm sorry about what my son said. I was ashamed and didn't know what to say, so I ran. I'm sorry about that too. It's my fault that I didn't teach him about people who look different. I bought a book that has people from different places in the world and am teaching him now that we all look different but we're the same."

I was happy that she came back and told me what she'd done. And I loved that she was teaching her child that race and color don't make up a person's character, but are things we can celebrate.

That was an important lesson for me to learn as well, because soon my attention fell on a young man I'd met at Calvin.

🌺 🌺 🌺 🌺 🌺

During my last semester, the international development studies department held a conference for its students, which included going off campus for a long weekend retreat. I didn't want to go, but one of my best friends, Karen, who was also studying international development, talked me into it.

The afternoon we were set to leave, all the students gathered on campus to take a bus together to the retreat site. As Karen and I sat on the bus waiting to depart, I looked at my watch. We were supposed to be gone already.

"What's the holdup?" I wondered aloud.

"Yeah, let's go!" a few people chimed in.

The leader shook his head. "Not yet. We're waiting for one more student, Jordan Roeda."

Finally this guy showed up. The department was fairly

small, so I thought I knew most of the students—or at least could recognize them—but I'd never set eyes on him before. He was white with wavy blond hair like a hippie surfer. On the surface, he looked like most of the other Dutch-American boys on campus, but there was something different about the way he held himself. He walked to the back of the bus and sat alone.

We arrived at a camp about forty-five minutes later and settled into our cabins before we reconnected for a welcoming get-together, first session, and dinner. At the get-together, people were chatting and getting to know one another better. My eye caught that same guy as he entered the room. He wore purplish-blue bell-bottom jeans and a white hoodie sweater with the hood up so that just a bit of his blond hair poked out around the edges.

Our first session included a former student who was out working in the real world. He was talking about some sort of development theory when the white-hoodie-sweatered guy spoke up. "I used to think that way," he said to the speaker. "But when I came back from Ghana last semester, my view totally switched on this theory." He began to share his thoughts.

I stared at him. I'd been annoyed by his tardiness, but now he grabbed my attention because I thought he was making sense. When we broke for dinner, he ate with some other people, so I didn't have an opportunity to ask him about his time in Ghana. After dinner, however, I took my plate to the sink to wash the dishes. He joined me and introduced himself.

The rest of the group was watching a video on a small television in the corner of the room.

"What are they watching?" I asked him.

"*The Princess Bride*," he said.

"I haven't seen it."

"It's like a fairy tale, but it parodies a lot of the clichés of the genre . . ."

He went on, but I wasn't really listening as much to what he was saying as to his voice. I liked it. It was gentle but firm. Soothing in its cadence.

"So you were in Ghana," I said after a while.

"Yes, I studied there last semester. Have you been to West Africa?"

"No."

"Oh, where are you from?" I'm sure he could tell from my accent that I wasn't originally an American.

"I'm from Sudan."

"Oh, okay. That's cool."

As I washed the dishes, he dried them and put them away. I was impressed by his helpfulness. This was something most men in my culture didn't do. Dinka men are traditionally prohibited from being in the kitchen.

He seemed easy to talk with, and I told him about the war and how I came to Michigan in 2000, and then how I ended up at Calvin. I didn't tell him about my daughter, not because of her but because of the circumstances surrounding everything. I didn't want to discuss what had happened to me with someone I'd just met. I couldn't believe how much I *was* telling him, though. He just kept smiling, listening, and asking more questions, giving me his complete attention. He was one of the best listeners I'd ever met. I didn't feel any judgment coming from him, which made me feel comfortable and appreciated. His blue eyes pierced me with their intensity.

But he was a junior. I was graduating in May and he still had another year to go. I sighed inwardly and doubted anything would come of this connection. After the retreat I thought we might not connect again, since I didn't have his contact information and we clearly never ran into each other on campus. But the interaction we'd had stayed with me. I looked him up on Facebook and decided to message him.

I was surprised and thrilled when he answered right away that it was good to see me and that we should definitely get together.

"Would you like to meet Thursday at Gojo?" he wrote. Gojo was an Ethiopian restaurant not far from campus. "I've never had Ethiopian food, but I'd like to try it. I'm free in the late afternoon and evening."

I read his message and my insides jumped up and down. He wanted to see me and share an African experience with me! Though I was tempted to respond right away, I didn't want to appear too forward, so I waited a day before getting back to him.

Let's just see how interested he is, I thought and smiled to myself.

The next day I wrote, "Okay, meeting in the evening

is better for me because I have busy afternoons on Thursdays. Would dinner at seven work for you?"

A response came back quickly. "Sounds good. Have a great night!"

That Thursday we met at Gojo and enjoyed our Ethiopian meal. It was fun to watch his expressions while he experienced the food. I could tell he really liked it.

Now was my time to dig deeper into who he was, so I asked him about himself and his family. He was studying international development, as I was, because he too wanted to make a difference in the world. But he was also combining it with a major in philosophy.

His grandparents left the American South because they felt called to missions in Latin America, so his dad grew up speaking Spanish and then continued on in mission work. His dad was a pastor and his parents were former missionaries. Jordan was born in the Dominican Republic when his parents were missionaries there. His family seemed pretty open to accepting different cultures, which surprised me because I assumed they had lived only in Western Michigan. Now I was even more intrigued.

"What would your family say if you dated someone from Africa?" I asked. I'd broken my rule about not being too forward, but I had to ask.

He looked at me thoughtfully. "I think they would understand."

Afterward we took a walk around Reeds Lake, a picturesque lake about ten minutes east of downtown Grand

Rapids. As we walked, our conversation continued to flow easily—until the subject of faith came up.

"I don't know how people can believe God is good," he said. "I'm frustrated with the church and with Christians. It seems like they make the Bible say whatever they want to believe. I'm not sure I can call myself a Christian anymore."

I almost stopped walking. "Why?"

"It seems like Christianity is a performance. When I went to Ghana, they read the Bible in a totally different way. Everyone came to different conclusions than the Christians I know here in the US. When I came back, everything just sounded hollow. It was like the Bible was being used to justify each personal agenda. If that's what Christianity is about, I don't want to be part of it."

"How can you say that? People are people. We're all broken and need God, but just because we are Christians doesn't make us perfect. We continue to work out our salvation—and sometimes we don't do that well. But God is still good. Christians sometimes do unthinkable things, but it doesn't mean there's no God or that he isn't good. If you stop believing in God because of what people do, you were never believing in God in the first place. You were believing in people."

He listened, but I could tell he didn't feel like he could believe it. That disappointed me. Even though I still felt a connection with him, I knew I couldn't pursue someone who didn't share a strong faith, because that was the most important thing to me.

We continued our friendship, going different places together and enjoying each other's conversation, but it seemed as if every time we got together, we argued over our faith. I tried to explain to him why he wasn't seeing things clearly. And he, being a philosophy major, kept throwing all kinds of arguments at me that I didn't know how to answer. All I knew was that I had lived a traumatic life and God had been present, sustaining and strengthening me through it all. Even when I was the angriest at God for allowing terrible things to happen to me, when my anger dissipated, I could see that in those darkest times, he was there, comforting me and working behind the scenes to redeem them. I'd lost my parents and my grandmother, the most important people in the world to me, and yet God brought me to the United States and gave me a new family and an education. I'd had a hardship happen to me, but in spite of that, Cholie was the best thing in my life. I still wasn't glad those horrific things had happened, but I could see God's handiwork redeeming them and making them into something ultimately very beautiful. I wanted Jordan to know that and to understand that God was doing the same in his life too.

I eventually began to understand that his struggles with faith were partially the consequence of reentry shock after his semester in Ghana. He had difficulty readjusting to his own culture, and his struggle with the problem of evil was, in part, an outgrowth of that. I prayed that he would continue to seek God and his direction for Jordan's life, because I knew no matter how hard I tried to persuade Jordan, only the Holy Spirit could convict and convince.

The summer of 2008 came and I graduated, while Jordan returned to his parents' home in Wisconsin. I spent time figuring out next steps for my future, and I discovered there was a scholarship for people who wanted to get a master's degree and return to Sudan to help rebuild the country. There was talk that Sudan would split in two— north and south. If it did, they would need educated men and women to help put things back together and create a new government in the southern part. Hope was high, especially in my Sudanese community. So I accepted the scholarship. I applied and was accepted to Grand Rapids Theological Seminary about ten minutes from Calvin. I decided to study ministry and organizational leadership, because it would be a good companion to international development. My studies would also focus on the faith aspect—hermeneutics and systematic theology. I wanted to make a difference in the world, but I wanted people to know about faith as well, since God is the only one who makes a true and lasting difference for the better.

While I was spending time back home with Cholie and my foster family, I received a suprising text from Jordan. "Can we meet up? I really need to talk to you."

He'd come back to town and taken a summer job.

"Of course," I texted him back, the thrill of seeing him again rising within me.

He'd gotten his hair cut and looked a little tan, although being white, there was only so much he *could* tan! Though he was still a stark contrast to my dark coloring, I didn't care. I was glad to see him and when I looked at him, I saw a beautiful man.

"Rebecca, I want you to know something," he told me when we got together. "I respect you and think you are smart and funny and fun to be around. And I think you're beautiful."

He said the words I'd always wanted to hear from a man—not so much that I was beautiful, though that was nice to hear, but that he respected me. Few men had told me this before. And here was this white, Dutch-American man telling me he respected me and cared about my thoughts and opinions.

He paused as though he were searching for the right words and then took my hand. "I want us to give this a chance. I want you to be my girlfriend."

I liked Jordan a lot too and respected him, and I figured this would just be a nice summer together, that nothing serious would develop. But still I felt the need to be honest with him about one thing. "You need to know, Jordan, that I'm not sure where this relationship will go, because it's important for me to be with someone who is strong in his faith."

He nodded his understanding.

As he walked me to my car afterward, I took a deep breath and turned to him. "There's something else you need to know about me." I paused. This would determine if he respected and accepted me as he said he did. If not, then he'd get into his car, drive away, and that would be the end of it.

"I have a daughter," I told him. "Her name is Cholie and she's seven years old. She's a big part of my life and I love her." I didn't share all the details; I still wasn't completely ready to expose everything to him, but I did want to be honest with him that a relationship with me was a package deal. He couldn't have me without loving and respecting Cholie too.

His eyes widened momentarily, as he took in this unexpected news, but then they filled with compassion. Again, he nodded his understanding. "I'd like to meet her—and the rest of your family," he said, and smiled kindly.

My heart filled with warmth toward this unusual and wonderful man.

The summer moved into the fall and winter, and though our relationship deepened, the issue of faith continued to bother Jordan. Both he and I were committed to our beliefs, and neither of us was willing to compromise them for the sake of this relationship.

At one point, he grew frustrated and asked me, "How can you believe God is good? You lost your parents. A war destroyed your country. Where was God in all of this?"

I let his words sink in. I didn't want to give a pat answer, because the question was a fair one. "You know, Jordan. You are studying international development because you want to help hurting people in the world. But when I was running in the war, we used to see UN workers in their Land Cruisers. They would get out and give us food, water, a ride, and take notes, and then get back in their vehicles and drive away. They didn't address issues of my heart, of mental health, when we felt unwanted and sad about what was happening to my people and how they were dying from the war, from starvation, from animals eating them, or even when we got attacked in the refugee camp by citizens of our host country. God's voice said, *'You are made in my image. I want you.'* When I think of not wanting to live anymore, God was the *only* one there for me then."

Jordan was quiet, but my answer still didn't seem to get through to him. Now I became frustrated with him. "You know what? If all of that hadn't happened to me, I never would have met you."

It was dark so I couldn't see Jordan's face clearly, but I heard a slight sniff and saw a twinkle of light by his eye that looked like a tear.

It felt as if we were at an impasse and I wasn't sure what to do. What I didn't realize was that God had used my words to reach Jordan's heart. Slowly Jordan began finding resolution to his questions. Shortly before we met, he'd told God that he was finished with trying to pursue him, and that the ball was now in God's court if he wanted a relationship. That was when he and I met. When I told Jordan that I never would have met him had those terrible things not happened to me, he realized that God had shown grace to him through my suffering. He didn't feel worthy of that, and was humbled to quietness before God at the mystery of suffering and grace. It forced him out of an intellectual and a philosophical approach to faith.

As our dating passed the one-year mark, I was grateful

we shared a faith foundation, not just because of who God is in our lives, but for another important reason: We were up against another serious obstacle—my Sudanese community, some of whom weren't likely to accept an interracial relationship.

CHAPTER 15

Though None Go with Me

He's *kawaja!*"

Some southern Sudanese members of the community were not happy about my relationship with Jordan. I'd started taking him with me to the Sudanese get-togethers, and as soon as they discovered we were together, they let their displeasure be known.

It wasn't that they were against Jordan because he was white; they were against the idea that he wasn't Dinka, and they feared that his family wouldn't accept me as a Dinka black woman. He couldn't carry on the traditions of the Dinka people, and if our relationship moved to marriage, I wouldn't carry on those traditions either. Tradition and being part of the community are everything to my people. I knew their arguments were coming from a place of fear. They worried that we might get married and then he would divorce me because being in an intercultural relationship would be too difficult. Some in my community even suggested that he or his community might mistreat me.

I struggled to figure out how best to help them understand that I wasn't turning on the Dinka way or on my people, it was just that someone special was in my life who understood me and shared my calling.

When Cholie and Aidan were kids, I watched a lot of movies with them, which helped me learn English. My favorite movie was *Winnie the Pooh*. In it Piglet asked, "How do you spell *love*?" Pooh answered, "You don't spell it, you feel it." When my Sudanese family questioned why I chose a poor American white man, risking being mistreated because of my color and culture, over all the educated, young Dinka men from good families, I told them I couldn't explain why I loved him, but all I could say was that I felt it, that he was the person I wanted to be on this journey with.

I tried to explain that it had nothing to do with race or color or tradition. When I was around him, I had a deep sense of peace and felt as though our souls had known each other for eternity.

But still they wouldn't understand. "You're rejecting a Sudanese man who knows your roots, one who will make your family proud. Why?"

No answer would satisfy.

By the summer of 2009, after I'd been at seminary for a year, a semester-long internship arose through Sudan Interior Mission (SIM) that would allow me to travel back to Sudan starting in the fall. I would travel to several villages where my role was to teach English, religion, and history to student teachers in their mission schools. It was now safe to return to Sudan, because the civil war had ended in 2005 when the government of Sudan and the

Sudan People's Liberation Movement, led by John Garang de Mabior, signed the Comprehensive Peace Agreement.

Peace had come and many who had fled their villages were returning to rebuild and start their lives over. I wanted to see my land again—the land I remembered as serene and beautiful. This would be the first time I'd returned since 1991. I hoped I'd be able to take a side trip to my village.

Before I left, though, Mum suggested that we travel to Scotland to visit her relatives there, and she encouraged Jordan to go with us. He'd already met my foster family and Cholie, and got along well with all of them, especially my daughter. I'd met his family and liked them immensely.

Jordan had never been to Scotland, so he quickly accepted the invitation. I thought it would be a fun trip, so I agreed too. The time would be right before my trip to Sudan, so I'd leave from Scotland and head straight there while my family and Jordan would return to the States.

We had a wonderful time visiting relatives and sightseeing, but I felt nervous around Jordan, as though I sensed he and my mum had conspired to get us there so Jordan could propose to me. But I wasn't ready.

One day while Jordan and I were alone, walking along a path around Loch an Eilein, a beautiful, clear lake in the Scottish Highlands of Aviemore with a castle in the center, not far from where the family was staying, I thought this might be it. I turned toward him to make a preemptive strike.

"Jordan, I know you love me and I love you. I think you

are a great guy. But I'm about to go to Sudan and I haven't been there since 1991. That's almost twenty years. I don't know the person I will be when I come back. I need to figure out who I am. Whatever has happened between us, I want to celebrate that. I want us to be happy right now. I don't want to do something before I say . . . well, if you were to ask me something."

I watched his face fall, but I pushed through.

"I will tell my family about dating you, though. I will be honest about it. I will tell them when I'm there, but I don't want to be like I'm dating *and* there's this too. Do you understand?"

He smiled kindly. "I understand. I think you should go home to Sudan and then we'll talk." Just as I'd told him about Cholie and watched him surprise me by staying committed to me, here he was again, showing me this setback wasn't going to chase him away either.

A couple days later, I flew to Nairobi. As we landed on a sunny afternoon, my thoughts went back to the trip I'd made from Kakuma. Nairobi had been our first layover on that long trip. How different I was now. I was an independent woman, educated, no longer malnourished or fearful.

My stepmother, Mama Atany, was living in Nairobi, so I planned to stay a week with her before traveling on to Sudan. She'd met up with us in Kapoeta during the war as we were fleeing and then separated from us, taking my half sisters Atong and Nyanguom with her. She'd lived for a time at the border of Uganda and Sudan, then lived in

Kakuma until Atong, who'd moved to Australia as a refugee, sent her money to move to Nairobi.

When I arrived I was overwhelmed by the welcome she planned for me. She invited friends from her church, Kenyan and Sudanese friends and neighbors, and relatives who were living in the area. They killed and cooked a goat and we celebrated my return. My relatives told me stories about my father and our family. Now as an adult, those stories were more precious than ever; I understood the important link to my past and what my parents and Kokok had sacrificed for me to live and to be free.

From there I flew to Juba, Sudan. The war had ended in 2005, and NGOs (non-governmental organizations) had done a lot of work in the city. It was like a new place holding so much promise. I visited some of my childhood friends who'd been in Kakuma with me but who now lived and worked there. It seemed as if peace had finally arrived and everyone talked about the southern part of Sudan becoming its own independent and free country. Hope was everywhere, and it filled my heart as well for these wonderful, innocent people who had been through so much tragedy.

From Juba I flew to Malakal, which is in the Upper Nile state in southern Sudan, and met up with Deborah, my roommate who was also on scholarship and who was also studying at Grand Rapids Theological Seminary. The school we were to teach at was not far from Malakal, but we had to take a boat on the White Nile to get there. It was evening when we left for the school. Deborah and I stepped on a long, metal boat filled with building materials and a cow. It was just light enough that we could see the surrounding reeds in the water, but not much else. Every now and then, we heard a splash and someone would say, "That's a hippo" or "That's a crocodile."

Hearing the splashes so close to the boat set me on edge.

"You afraid?" one of the boatmen asked. "You're American. You are afraid. It's okay. Sometimes the hippos tip the boat, but that's okay; we turn it back over and you just get back in."

That didn't make me feel better!

When we arrived at Atar, the village where the school was, people rushed from everywhere to greet us. They were Dinkas but they had different accents. I had to pay close attention to what they were saying to understand them, even though I spoke the same language.

I was delighted to see some girls I knew from Kakuma. They had been in group thirty-four, not far from my group. When the war ended, they returned. Now they were learning to be teachers.

For the next two weeks Deborah and I taught English training, sort of like ESL, to students who came from all over southern Sudan. Our training helped them return to their villages and teach what they'd learned. I loved every minute of it. I was part of helping my people get educated. When the students saw that we too had learned English, it offered them real hope and a dream to give their people in their villages.

While everyone had much to celebrate with the end of the civil war four years before, they were still carrying its devastation. The countryside that I remembered as so green, beautiful, and clean was littered with the remnants of mortar shells and bullet casings. People were still rebuilding their villages, but I could see huts that had been scorched or garbage lying around, things I'd never seen before the war.

One night while some women and I were collecting wildflowers by the river, we heard gunfire in a distant village. Immediately the easygoing atmosphere turned tense and fearful.

"Let's go!" one of the women shouted and started to run.

"Where are we running to?" I asked, following her, all the emotions of fleeing my village so many years ago returning in an instant.

We ran back to the village, but I wasn't sure that would be safe. What if that was where the gunfire was coming from? Everybody in the village had heard it too and was running around scared and disoriented. Men were on high alert, holding guns and weapons ready to fight. Women and children were hiding in the huts or running toward the forest.

Soon we heard news that somebody was just drunk in a neighboring village and was shooting off his gun. Everyone seemed to exhale together.

"Even though peace has come, we don't take it for granted," one of the villagers told me. "It's been too long living under fear of death and war. We never know when the northern government might break their word and begin fighting and killing again."

One of the elder ladies told me, "You know a long time ago when we traveled, we used to be afraid of animals like lions or hyenas or something attacking you, but now we don't worry about those things as much. When we are walking and we see a human being, we are afraid."

After we finished the training, Deborah and I left Atar village to travel to Yabus, in the southern Blue Nile region, to teach there. While I enjoyed my work, I found I missed Jordan. We Skyped or emailed as often as we could, even though the internet was often down. Unfortunately, we went through a two-month period where I had no access, so we didn't communicate with each other, and I missed him terribly.

Our SIM compound had internet, though, so Jordan and I would instant message each other as often as we could. For some reason, however, as soon as I got started, the internet would go out. What I didn't realize was that one of the guys who operated it liked me and disliked the idea that I was involved with someone else, so he would "accidentally" knock out the access.

I was one of the Lost Girls who had returned home and had gotten an education, which made me a person of status. Knowing my father was a general in the SPLA also brought me great status, so a lot of men showed up wanting my hand in marriage.

I rolled my eyes at it. I wasn't interested in any courtship. I thought it fascinating that I'd come home to find myself, and I found that I liked who I was with Jordan. He was patient and kind. He was romantic, writing me poetry and telling me how much he loved me and how he was praying for me. He always asked how I was doing and how the environment was. He supported my being there and the work I felt called to do. Those times of connection were always so special, and I wished he were there to experience Sudan with me.

Someday, I told myself, and the thought filled me with hope.

"I think I've found the one," I told Deborah. "I think I'm going to marry Jordan. It's just become clear to me that this is the man God has been preparing for me."

She smiled and nodded, as though she already knew.

Toward the end of my time there, moving into the end of November, I went to see some family. My mom's brothers lived in Bor, and the last time they saw me I was one year old and my mother was still alive. When I arrived, my mother's childhood friends were there to greet me. They led me to the rest of my family and we sat and drank tea and talked. A woman walked in, looked around the group, and asked, "When is the daughter of Achol coming?"

One of my cousins pointed at me. "She is sitting right there."

The woman walked over to me and looked me straight in the eyes, then she shook her head. "Ooh, how could my best friend give birth to *this* girl? She is a photocopy of her father and has nothing to do with Achol. I can't believe she doesn't look anything like our princess Achol." She shook her head again and grunted. "The womb can produce anything it likes."

I was stunned. I had often heard how I was not beautiful like my mother, but this woman took it to another level.

"Well, come," she said, holding out her hand for me. She walked me to sit by the other women. "We have a funny story to tell you about your mother when she was young."

I leaned in to hear it. I'd heard so few stories about my mother, so I was sure to treasure this one.

"Did you know your mother's nickname was Buffalo Balls' Grabber?"

What in the world is this woman talking about? Is she drunk? I looked around at the other women who were nodding and smiling.

"One day when she was a child at a cattle camp, some of the teen boys were trying to hunt a buffalo, only the buffalo began chasing them. Everybody panicked and ran away. Everybody except your mother. She ran right toward that buffalo, dove under it, and grabbed his balls. That gave the men an opportunity to regroup and spear the buffalo, but they didn't want to hurt your mother, who was still holding on tight! They went after its shoulders and forehead until it finally went down. Everybody talked about your mother from that day on. She was known as the girl who went after a buffalo's balls! That became her nickname, especially when people teased her or when they referred to her bravery. They'd say, 'Hi, Buffalo's Balls!' "

We all laughed at the story, but it was more than just a funny tale to me. *That's where I got my bravery—from my mother.* It gave me a connection to her that I needed.

After the laughter died down, the women sighed and frowned slightly. I could tell they were thinking the same thing I was: *I miss her.*

"Your mother was beautiful," another woman said. "Before she became a teenager, she already had five men who wanted to marry her. Your grandfather Riak Gong and your grandmother Ayen Ajuong loved her very much. They'd had children who had died and were broken-hearted over it. Your mother was their last child, and they named her Achol, which means 'God redeemed the lost by giving new life and mending a broken heart.' "

I wished I had more time to spend with my mother's family and friends to hear more stories, but too soon I had to leave. It was time to see Uncle Machok. So from Bor my cousin Dhieu drove me to one of the villages in the Duk Payuel area, which was close to where Uncle Machok was now living in Duk Padiet. We drove for a day and a half, traveling mostly at night because it was cooler and less dangerous. But I wasn't sure it was all that safe. We traveled over treacherous roads, almost hitting a family of hyenas, getting threatened by some soldiers who wanted us to pay a toll to travel a road, and almost breaking down. But when we arrived at the village, Poktap, Uncle wasn't there. He had a phone, so I called to find out when I could see him. He was staying in a neighboring village, but was planning to come the next day.

"Actually, Uncle, why don't I come to see you? Then we could go to my village."

"No, I will come to you. We won't be able to travel to the village," he said.

Disappointment washed over me. I'd traveled all this way and really wanted to go there, where I'd left Kokok. I imagined walking back and seeing her exit from her hut and smile at me, still very much alive and well. I hoped to revisit the smells, scenery, and Kokok's pasture, hoping perhaps I'd recognize something.

When I mentioned it to my cousins, they agreed with my uncle. "No, you don't want to go there right now. A few soldiers are still stationed in the area and it might not be safe getting there," they said. "There's not much there to see anymore anyway, since nobody's lived in the village since 1991 and it is a thick forest now." My heart ached.

Later that day other relatives began to show up. Mama Nyadak, who was married to my uncle Chuol, ran toward me, shouting, "Where is my child? Where is my child?" She threw her arms around me and hugged me so tightly I could barely breathe. She began singing and crying about how happy she was that I was safe and home. "How powerful is God that he allows me to see you again! We've lost so much!"

I began to cry too, I was so touched by her display of affection and pain. She had been captured during the war that destroyed our village and had only recently been released and returned to the area.

She continued to hug me and cry, until somebody yelled, "Nyadak, please! She is alive, not dead, so let us celebrate instead of crying and being sad."

"Come," she said, taking my hand and leading me to sit next to her. Someone brought us tea and we sipped while she chatted away. "Do you remember me, my daughter? You were so little when I last saw you! But look at you now. If I met you in a crowd, I would not know you, but I have heard so much about you. You are doing well. I am proud."

The next morning I asked if I could shower to get ready for the day. One of the women took a container of water to a small open area with a cement floor, surrounded by tall woods. This reminded me of Kakuma, except there was no pit hole next to it for the toilet. I started putting water on my body using my hands, which reminded me that I hadn't done that for a long time. I had forgotten the art of holding water in my hands so I could clean my body. I was home in Sudan, but I was now American.

Later that day Uncle Machok arrived. "Welcome back, WunAjang!" he said, using my nickname.

I threw my arms around him and studied him. He looked older. His hair had patches of gray throughout now. But he'd made it back to Sudan and seemed happier about life than when I left him at Kakuma Refugee Camp. We talked and caught each other up on our lives. He'd left the camp in 2007 and found work building schools. His job was to cut down trees and prepare the land. He liked it;

it gave him purpose and something to do at his village for his people.

As more and more relatives showed up, they killed a bull and cooked it so we could celebrate my return. Everyone wanted to hear how I was doing and was pleased when I told them I was doing well and not only finished school but had graduated from college and was getting a master's degree.

They knew I hadn't married and several asked about when I was going to settle down with a good Dinka man. I avoided the question as much as I could, unsure of what or how much to say. But I'd been raised to respect and honor my elders, so I knew I needed to tell them the truth.

"I have to talk to you about something," I told them, surprised by how my voice shook. "I am dating an American man, and we are serious. I think I'm going to marry him."

They were all quiet for a long time.

When I could take the silence no longer, I said, "Do you have anything to say?"

My uncle said, "What happened to the man you liked at Kakuma, Tongwut? I heard he had moved to the US."

I nodded. "It didn't work out."

"And in all the US, all the Dinka men there, there's nobody it can work out with?"

"Well, I didn't date all of them, but..." I chuckled to try to lighten the mood.

"What do you mean by date?"

"Oh." I'd forgotten that Dinkas practice long courtships in which they check the man's background when they find a good family with a good family name.

"Are you for sure saying this thing? Or is it not true?" my uncle asked after another very long pause.

"It's true."

"No, it's not true. You'll have to tell us something else." He, Uncle Luk, Dhieu, and my other relatives looked away as the atmosphere became more and more awkward, until Dhieu kicked my foot and whispered, "You need to change the topic."

What do I say now? I told them the truth, and they don't want to hear it.

He looked at me, as if pleading for me to do something, but I didn't know what to do.

"Ha! Rebecca, did you not tell me that your cousin in the US said it would be funny to tell your uncle you're marrying a white man?" He laughed.

I paused for a moment and then smiled. "Yeah, yeah!" I knew I had to play along.

Immediately everybody started to laugh. "That was a very funny joke! Haha, Rebecca marrying a white man! What a good joke to play on us."

With the tension gone, everybody reverted to chatting and laughing in their easy way.

The next day was my time to leave. As I got ready to go, my uncle came to me. "I know you," he said quietly. "The thing you said last night was not a joke, was it?"

I smiled. "No."

He nodded his understanding, but he didn't return my smile. "Well, you go back to the US. You call me and we'll talk about it."

"Okay, Uncle. And thank you."

I saw my mother's relatives one more time in Bor, then returned to Nairobi to stay a couple days with my stepmother. While I was there, I received a phone call from one of my friends back in the States. I was surprised to hear from him.

"Rebecca, how are you doing?" he asked.

"Good, I'm doing good." I told him my family and I had just finished eating and were laughing and reminiscing.

He paused as if confused. "Oh, well, I just sent you a hundred and fifty dollars through Western Union, and I want to give you the confirmation number."

Now I was confused. "Why did you send me money? I don't need money."

"I sent it because of the bad news in your family and so you guys can help."

"What bad news?"

"You haven't heard? Your uncle Machok was killed two days ago in the village."

The phone slipped from my hand and dropped to the floor. My world was collapsing all over again.

My stepmother grabbed the phone and yelled into it. "Who is this? What has happened? What did you say to her?"

I could hear him repeat the news, and she began to scream.

I learned later that while he was cutting trees to build a school in the village, six men showed up and attacked him with machetes. They were brutal in their attack, leaving him in pieces.

That night I called the airline and changed my flight so I could stay an extra day. In the Dinka culture when somebody dies, we have an assembly where we eat together and talk. So the next day, our relatives from the area gathered. They killed another goat to eat, and people came and wept and prayed.

What had started as such an exciting adventure, in which I returned to my homeland filled with the joy of helping my people and getting reacquainted with my relatives, ended in tragedy yet again. Uncle Machok was one of only two living brothers of my father, out of a total of six, and he was the link I had to my past, who knew about my baba and kokok, who had been with me through the flight from our village, who had given me a chance to leave an engagement flag hanging at our hut in Kakuma and let me leave for the United States, and who had promised that we would talk in a few days after I returned to the US. Now he too was gone. I'd lost another loved one to violence.

I spent the flight back to the States mourning everything that had been taken from me. I wept over my uncle's death, but also over so many things that his death took with him. I felt lost all over again. I just wanted to get to the Grand Rapids airport and throw myself into my foster parents' arms. But when I arrived, they weren't there. They were running late and couldn't get hold of me to tell me.

I crumpled into a chair and sobbed. *I don't even have a home!* I thought, my emotions taking over. *Nobody's even here to pick me up on time.*

I felt emotionally spent, but then I got mad. *I went to Sudan to try to help them build a better country. And what happens? They take the one person, the only one who knew me!*

I'd had enough and I didn't want to hear anything from Sudan—not even one of my family members. They'd let me down and now I wasn't going to bother worrying what they thought or wanted. And if Jordan asked me to marry him, I was going to say yes—without apology or seeking my family's approval.

※ ※ ※ ※ ※

I returned from Sudan in early January 2010, and Jordan proposed in March. I was happy and in love with him so of course I said yes, because I knew I wanted to be with him.

I called my half brother Luk, who was now living in Lansing, Michigan, and told him about my engagement. He asked where my fiancé was from in southern Sudan. When he learned that my fiancé wasn't Dinka, he said simply, "Okay."

After I hung up, I wasn't hurt. I was confident Luk would come to like Jordan once he got to know him. There was no doubt in my mind that all my relatives would love Jordan too. But some stubbornly refused.

"You know you really found the poorest white man in America, and he's just a boy," one person said. "He has no money to pay dowry. Why would we give away one of our educated girls to such a poor boy?"

One man tried to outbid Jordan's proposal, saying, "I will outbid this guy. Whatever he brings, I've got more cows." It was as though the community was trying to save me from this thief who was stealing me away from the Dinka way of life or saving me from myself because I didn't know what I was doing.

I felt badly for Jordan more than anything. He didn't deserve to be treated that way. He was concerned about what my family in Sudan had to say about us. I told him that before Uncle Machok died, he was supportive of us getting married. Even though that wasn't exactly true, I didn't want to burden Jordan with that. And I was trying to reconcile his last words to me. I knew Uncle was open to talking more about it, but that didn't mean he supported it.

I wanted to be happy—and I wanted my family to be happy for us, so it hurt that they were unbudging. According to Dinka culture, I always learned that what makes a person different is his or her heart, not race. When I was growing up, Uncle Machok told me that the heart was the most important thing. Uncle Machok would say, "Do you know that all the people in the world have one race? Their hearts! When you speak the truth or the language that the heart understands, the outside differences don't stand a chance." He'd said when looking for a person to marry, the most important thing was that the person had integrity and came from a family of dignity—and that was Jordan.

It spotlighted my dilemma. I was Sudanese in culture, but no longer a citizen of that country. I was American, but not culturally American. How could I ask Jordan to accept me when I was no longer sure who I was or where I belonged?

Our engagement *was* an exciting time for me, but deep down, I was also still reeling from my uncle's death. I felt depressed and didn't know how to talk or where to begin. I didn't know how to process or mourn.

A lot of people welcomed me home and said, "That's so great that you were able to go back to Sudan and connect with your roots." I just answered, "Yeah, it was good" and left it at that. I didn't have the energy or desire to share that my uncle had been murdered. What could they have said anyway?

As I sank deeper into depression, I found myself questioning God again, because nothing made sense. "Why did you take me there?" I prayed. But God didn't answer.

One day I felt a nudge to look through my journal from the trip. As I flipped through the pages, scanning the entries I made while I was wrapping up my teaching in Yabus and before I went to Dinka land to visit relatives, I found prayers about Uncle Machok.

"I know there have been a lot of attacks in the area where he's now living," I wrote. "But please keep him for me so I can see him. And even if he dies, let me see him before that. Let me see him one more time."

I sat back in my chair and stared at my writing. I'd prayed, and God had answered. And now I was upset with him because he'd allowed something to happen that I couldn't understand. But yet he *had* clearly answered my prayers.

I whispered through tears, "Even when I don't under-stand and when bad things happen, I know you still care for us. Bad people killed my uncle. Evil people who do not know you killed my uncle. You didn't kill my uncle."

My prayer didn't take the ache away, but slowly a peace settled over me.

CHAPTER 16

Working Toward Peace and Healing

Rebecca, I have an opportunity I think you'd be perfect for," my friend Mayak told me over the phone in December 2010. He explained that southern Sudan was holding a referendum on whether or not the South should split from the North and form its own country. "It's going to be a worldwide vote, so they're looking for Sudanese people to run the voting center in Washington, DC." He had heard about it through the International Organization for Immigration (IOM), one of the project implementers.

My heart skipped a beat. That would mean independence for my homeland. No longer would they have to be fearful of the northern Sudanese soldiers and militias invading villages and killing or exploiting innocent people of the South.

And I can be directly involved? I thought. *This is a dream come true!*

I was in my final year at seminary, set to graduate in May 2011, and Jordan and I had set our wedding date for the following month. I put together my résumé and submitted it. Soon I was packing my bags and heading for Alexandria, Virginia, just outside Washington.

A lot of the Lost Boys were talking in the media and to the US government about all the suffering still continuing back home. For years the US Congress listened to our stories, and President George W. Bush was instrumental in encouraging the signing of the Comprehensive Peace Agreement in 2005, which laid the groundwork for a referendum to take place. In September 2010, in an address to the United Nations, President Barack Obama then encouraged the referendum process to proceed so the southern Sudanese people could have a right to decide our homeland's fate.

The referendum in the United States, or what they called "out of the country voting," was set to take place January 9 through 15, 2011, but they wanted to have leaders set well before then to get everything ready and to contact as many members of the south Sudanese diaspora as they could. Since so many people had left Sudan during the war, the referendum needed to be worldwide.

The United States would have eight voting centers—Boston, DC, Chicago, Nashville, Dallas, Omaha, Phoenix, and Seattle. My job was to manage the DC voting center, which included overseeing sixty-five workers who were assigned to describe the referendum, register people to vote, and explain how the voting process worked. They also had to do their due diligence to make sure those who claimed to be from southern Sudan actually were. South

Sudanese communities then orchestrated transporta-
tion to get the thousands of people to and from the voting
center.

The hours were long; I sometimes worked thirteen- to
sixteen-hour days. I didn't mind because while doing this
work, I felt close to my father. He had fought using guns
and warfare to bring freedom to his people; I was using
my voice and vote. Bullets had brought no peaceful resolution, but I was carrying on his legacy, and hopefully I
would see the resolution come to pass so that he—and all
the others—wouldn't have died in vain.

By January, hope was high, but everyone was tense. The
UN, the IOM, the State Department, and the Carter Center observers showed up at the voting center to make sure
no one tried to sabotage or rig the outcome. They wanted
to make sure everything was secure and accurate; it would
be a fair vote.

Busloads of people showed up every day for seven days
from 9 a.m. to 6 p.m. It was a proud time for all south
Sudanese people—for the first time they had a voice in
determining their future and country. Some were crying
as they voted, some singing, some waving the SPLA flag—
with its golden morning star in the middle—and some
waving American flags.

We counted each vote in a high-security room while
UN, IOM, and US officials double-checked them all.

When the time came for me to cast my vote, I stood in
the voting booth and looked down at the simple yes-or-no
question. Did I vote for southern Sudan to become its own

country, with its own government, and its own right to choose how its people would live?

I smiled as I eagerly checked yes.

After seven days of voting and counting, the final tally was in. We knew how our center had done, but we had to wait to hear word from the rest of the voting centers around the world—from Australia, the UK, Denmark, Canada, Kenya, and of course southern Sudan.

When the time came for the outcome to be announced, my coworkers and I stood in the referendum offices, holding our breath. My body felt tense.

"Nearly ninety-nine percent of people voted yes for independence," the UN worker stated. South Sudan would officially become the world's newest country on July 9, 2011.

As my coworkers began cheering, I felt my knees go weak.

"We are independent. We are South Sudan. The star of the SPLM has led us home! The morning star did it. It is a new day!" people were chanting.

My chest heaved, and the walls felt as though they were about to cave in on me. I needed to leave the room, to escape. As quickly as I could, I raced down the hall and ran into the ladies' restroom, which was empty. I headed to the last stall, where I locked the door behind me and stood for a moment breathing hard.

Then the emotional dam broke. I wept as I'd never wept before. "Thank you, my ancestors. Thank you, God. Thank you!"

With each sob I spoke the name of a loved one who had died because of that evil, horrific war. "Baba, Mom, Kokok, Uncle Machok, my baby sister Akon..."

On and on the names poured into my mind and out onto my tongue. These people had either died from guns or famine or disease or animal attacks or sexual or physical abuse that were all connected to the war. "We didn't fail you! We finished the fight. Baba, we finished the fight!"

Then I began to call out the names of my heroes, those who had fought and given everything for freedom. "Baba, Uncle Deng Paul Awel, Wuor Arop, Deng Nhial, and our founding father, John Garang de Mabior..."

Every emotion I'd held in for almost two decades came spewing out—the sadness of what I'd experienced, of Uncle Machok's murder, which I was still grieving—but all the happiness too, like my engagement and my time with Jordan and my daughter, Cholie. As I stood in that stall and wept, all of those things that seemed so heavy in my body lifted, and for the first time I felt truly light. I was happy. My people were free. They could live as they wanted—following their beliefs—and they could choose for themselves and be independent for the first time.

As my tears slowly subsided, I began to hear people singing. It was a song we sang during the war about courage and perseverance, and I began to hum along.

The land hath destroyed us;
the land hath taken away our dignity;

but be strong women.
The orphan son and daughter,
they will live in freedom.
So women, be strong.

🌸 🌸 🌸 🌸 🌸

I returned to Michigan to focus now on graduating and preparing for my wedding. All the details seemed to fall easily in place . . . except for my family. The status of our native country may have changed, giving us freedom to choose our lives, but that didn't mean the culture had. While some in my Sudanese family and community wanted to bless my marriage to Jordan, some were still against it. Though they admitted they liked him as a person, they didn't believe he was the right choice for me.

A few days before the wedding, I began to receive calls from people making threats. "We're not coming to the wedding. Nobody will be there."

I began to shake. *Why can they not understand that I love Jordan?* I thought, feeling anxious. They just saw him as another American. I saw his heart. He loved me, he loved my daughter, and he loved God. Could they really think that wasn't enough?

Aunt Akararia, a member of the community, got wind of what was happening and came to see me. "See this through," she told me, smiling kindly. "Someday they will understand."

The next day, June 18, was a beautiful, sunny day in

Holland, Michigan—the perfect day for a wedding. My foster dad got teary-eyed as he stood at the back of the church with me.

"I'm so proud of you, Rebecca," he said.

As we walked down the aisle, I scanned the audience and could see that some of my family members were missing. I held back my tears. For the first time, regardless of being an orphan, I felt the deep shame of being disowned by my blood relatives. But God was faithful again to me. Many people did come. One uncle, Uncle Dut Bethou, stood during the reception and announced, "I speak for the whole family when I say that we accept Jordan and approve of this wedding." I wanted to run over to him and hug him! And later during the reception, Aunt Aker and Aunt Monica congratulated us and encouraged us to keep tight to our love for each other. Simon Chop, Mayom Bol, and several other of my cousins talked to Jordan and affirmed him.

Even with some of my family's absence, the wedding was beautiful and a wonderful celebration. We had American dancing and Dinka dancing—even Jordan's grandmother surprised us by taking to the dance floor with one of my uncles to the beat of the Dinka drums.

A few weeks after the wedding, I called my relatives in Kakuma Refugee Camp and South Sudan to tell them I got married. They seemed supportive and congratulated me. They also told me they received money that Jordan had sent so that they too could celebrate our wedding. (I was so proud of my new husband.) My cousin Dhieu, who covered for me when I told Uncle Machok about Jordan, told me, "I am happy for you. Your uncle knew you well, he knew that you were serious. And he knew that when you were serious about a thing, nobody would change your mind. Even though he died before he could talk with you more about it, you know he would eventually agree with you because he knew you."

His words about my uncle warmed my heart and comforted my soul.

🐾 🐾 🐾 🐾 🐾

Within a few months of our marriage, I heard about another opportunity to work with USAID, an organization that funds programs for education and peace building in underdeveloped countries. But it was an unpaid internship in Washington, DC. I applied and got accepted, thrilled that I could continue to work with Sudan and South Sudan.

Jordan and I packed everything we owned, which wasn't much, into our car, and headed to DC certain that with our education we would quickly find jobs. I enjoyed the internship, but when it ended, I was no further ahead in my career. Jordan worked some temporary jobs, including babysitting for a friend's six-month-old son.

Even though the months of job searching felt like years, God remained faithful. Jordan was able to get a job working in diversity and inclusion with the American Dental Education Association, but I still had nothing. I knew God had called me to this work, and I knew he would be faithful, but I began to wonder what was going on with my own career. Though I had years of real-world experience as a beneficiary of the programs I'd been part of in DC and I had a degree in my field, I wasn't considered qualified even for an entry-level position with any of the large development agencies working in Africa.

To add to the stress, we ran into our first real prejudice. One evening while Jordan and I were taking a walk, we saw a group of teenagers on the sidewalk ahead of us. We noticed that other people crossed the street to avoid the group.

I can't believe people are judging these kids because of their color, I thought.

As Jordan and I continued walking toward them, one of the girls said, "Dirty Dark Skin, go back to Africa, where you came from." The rest of the group laughed as they started inching their way toward us.

"Come on, guys," Jordan said, trying to keep things from escalating.

The group appeared threatening and we found no easy way to extricate ourselves from the situation, so I pulled out my phone and called the police.

But long minutes passed without the police arriving. Finally, Jordan called. Within minutes two officers showed up. They came quickly, which left me wondering, *Why when I called, nobody came, but when Jordan called two officers showed up immediately?*

It broke my heart to see these kids acting the way they did, but it also broke my heart that it seemed as though the police didn't feel my call was important enough for them to come to my aid. It took my white husband's call to get them to act.

Always, there is still so much work to be done.

🌺 🌺 🌺 🌺 🌺

By Thanksgiving 2012, we returned to Holland to celebrate the holiday with our family. Still unemployed, I felt unsure where I fit or belonged.

A friend from Holland, Kathy, called me while I was home, and told me about a woman who worked at American Bible Society (ABS). "Her name is Jane Jelgerhuis, and she lives in Holland," she said. "Give her a call while you're in town." Then she gave me Jane's phone number.

Jane and I clicked immediately. She was easy to talk with, she listened compassionately to my story, and the most surprising part was that she worked with American Bible Society's brand-new international program focusing on trauma healing for women from war-torn African countries, called She's My Sister.

The program uses a series of lessons about suffering that helps people give voice to what they've been through and then works through Scripture along with a mental health overlay of expertise, with the goal to help them experience wholeness and hope for new beginnings.

As soon as I heard about the program, my eyes lit up with excitement. "Yes, yes!" I told her. I remembered something I'd read from Dr. Diane Langberg, so I quoted it. "'I know that food can be grown as part of development.

Water can be purified. But who can heal the wounds of the heart?' That's the aspect of development I want to be involved with."

She agreed, and not long after our meeting, I received a call that American Bible Society wanted to hire me as a consultant advocate until a full-time position opened. My role was program development, working alongside those who train the program's facilitators in the Great Lakes Region of Africa, which includes Rwanda, Burundi, Democratic Republic of the Congo, Uganda, Republic of Congo, Tanzania, Central Africa Republic, Zambia, Kenya, Sudan, and South Sudan.

Jordan and I began finding our way in DC, but my mind was focused on my daughter. We began talking of moving back to Holland to be close to Cholie and my family. We also wanted to start a family and knew we could never do that in DC because of the high cost of living there. But if we left, were we quitting too soon?

What was worse was that another war had broken out in South Sudan. In December 2013, President Salva Kiir, who was Dinka, accused Riek Machar, a Nuer and former vice president, of attempting a coup. In the beginning of the war, I had said that I wished the two men would get into the fighting ring and whoever wanted to fight could join them in the ring, because I knew that the war would make all sides—right or wrong—suffer, especially those without resources. Everything we'd worked so hard for—the long hours of getting people to vote on a referendum that would provide independence to a hurting people—now seemed all for nothing as we heard about more deaths and violence, including more death for my family members and friends. I felt ashamed that my people turned on one another again and were killing themselves. And my heart broke knowing that another war meant there would be more Lost Boys and Lost Girls.

I trudged to the bedroom and sat on the edge of the bed with my eyes closed. In and out I breathed, no longer wanting to live, tired of carrying the burden of everything that had happened to me. I'd experienced such freedom and joy after the referendum and our wedding, yet it didn't last and the painful memories returned with a vengeance.

Even God seemed silent. Where was he now? Why didn't he just remove all of my lingering trauma? And why were the innocent Nuer and Dinka being massacred?

As my mind went haywire with confusing thoughts and an inability to focus, feeling as though I was drowning, hot tears rolled down my cheeks. I lay there for a while, until I realized I needed to face my demons and put my life back together. *What am I thinking? I've been so blessed. I have a beautiful daughter, a wonderful family, and a loving husband who cares so much for me. God is still faithful. He will take care of our needs.*

I called my husband, who was at work, and then I called my best friend, Karen. I needed encouragement, I told them. I needed community; I couldn't fight depression alone. Talking to both of them helped me see that I wasn't hopeless and that sometimes we all experience bumps along the path to achieving our calling.

I made myself some tea and took a walk to a nearby

park, where I sat on one of the benches and thought about my life. At that moment I decided I would no longer pray for a job or money for us to live comfortably. I decided I would only pray thanksgiving prayers, focusing my mind on all the ways God had provided and thanking him for what he would continue to do in my future.

Not long after that, God's timing and provision became apparent in an unexpected way. I felt as though I needed to go through the trauma program to experience what the women would experience. The program itself contained eleven lessons that focused on different aspects of trauma and healing. Since I worked alongside the trainer, I felt I should go through the material so I'd know what I would be helping with in the training.

Even though my foster father was a clinical psychologist who had worked with a lot of refugees, and he and my mum helped me process much of my pain, it wasn't until I went through the program myself that I began to recognize how truly wounded and chronically traumatized I'd been. I kept thinking, *I wish I'd been able to go through this program when I was younger, struggling so much with my experiences, and wondering whether God truly was all good.* I learned how to grieve, question, take my pain to the cross of Jesus, and ultimately to forgive.

I realized that what I'd experienced and felt for all those years wasn't crazy. Trying to adapt in the midst of ongoing trauma and trying to find a way while different cultures were telling me different things, it was easy to wonder, *What is wrong with me?* Those lessons showed me that nothing was wrong with me. It was human for my heart to feel sad over the inhumane ways I'd been treated and how people treated one another. It was okay for me to know that though I could never go back to the innocence of my childhood in my village, I could overcome the pain by acknowledging the problem and building resiliency.

Going through those lessons made my faith blossom, and I felt true healing take place. And the most beautiful part was that I saw healing not only within myself but also within the facilitators I worked with. I loved hearing them say, "God makes sense to me now. I feel for the first time that I can be mad at God and not be seen as evil. I can truly grieve and be okay."

I loved the work and seeing how it was changing the facilitators' lives, knowing that they would, in turn, help bring healing to the women and children of their communities who so desperately needed it.

In 2015 I returned to South Sudan to help lead children's trauma healing training in Juba, the country's capital. Although I didn't have the opportunity to visit family, I was grateful that the work I was doing could make a real impact on the lives of women and children throughout the country. It was great to see all the South Sudanese come together under the leadership of the Bible Society of South Sudan to provide one-week training to their local leaders to care for their communities. They desperately wanted to see healing come to the land.

I felt overwhelmed by the stories I heard that week, many so similar to mine, but others more horrific than I could have imagined. I heard stories of people sitting by the river and watching headless bodies float by, only to realize those were family members, or having to leave bodies where they lay for the birds, animals, and insects to bury them, or experiencing rape and displacement as a tool of war, or listening to grown men talk about being an invisible child or a child soldier, ripped from the safety of a loving family and village. I had seen and experienced so much, and yet listening, I realized how much Uncle Machok had protected me by not allowing me to see so much death from the war as we were escaping, and for that I was grateful. No child should witness war; no boy or girl should lose the innocence of childhood because of the trauma of war and its consequences.

As we went through the lessons during that week, we were all moved to see healing begin to take place. The exercise of "bring your pain to the cross" was especially poignant. It's a ceremony in which the students write down their grief, doubts, and questions about God and his goodness, as well as listing all the places they've been harmed. They fold the list and then attach it to a large cross at the front of the room, symbolizing that Jesus takes all our sorrows and pain and he washes them clean. At the end of the exercise, we burn all the papers to show that we put them completely into God's hands. Going through the exercise doesn't mean we never have hardships again, yet we are reminded that in Jesus we have true freedom and he will guide us and care for us always.

During that part of the exercise, an elderly man who lived internally displaced in Juba began to cry. "As a sinner to come before God and give him my pain is so overwhelming to me," he said. "By God's grace, we are saved, and that is what the nation of South Sudan needs. To forgive one another for wrongdoing because Christ forgave us first."

At the closing ceremony, I was amazed to watch the students' faces, shining and happy, as they received their one-week certificates.

One student, John Luka, came to me afterward and told me that this training had changed him and he looked forward to sharing with others so they could be changed too.

Being part of the training and hearing so many stories of healing from the South Sudanese allowed me to continue grieving my losses. I mourned Uncle Machok. Before, even though I'd cried over his death, I'd harbored anger at the barbaric way he had been taken—leaving only pieces for my relatives to bury. I spent time grieving my lost childhood, my lost village, and my lost family. Yet there was still one person I hadn't fully grieved—Kokok.

While attending a She Is Free conference in New York in 2016, we sang, "I'm not a slave to fear. I'm a child of God." Something stirred within my heart and Kokok's face came to my mind. I still missed her, even though I had never mourned her death, had never cried over that loss.

I felt an intense need to leave the conference and go up to my hotel room. As soon as I walked in my room, the tears came. For two hours straight I sobbed out all my grief over losing the person who had loved me so much when I was a child, who took me in when my mother died and made me her own, who had willingly sacrificed her life so I could survive.

I was no longer a child of Kokok, but as the tears slowly drained and I thought again of that song, I realized that I am no longer a slave to fear. I am a child of the almighty God, the Creator of heaven and earth, who sees me and loves me. I am a child of the God who healed me and who seeks to end war and bring peace and healing to all of creation, and who has called me to help in that important work—and part of that work is to let others know they too are a loved child of God.

CHAPTER 17

No Longer Lost

I think the baby is coming!" I cried to Jordan over the phone.

He had just left for work on a snowy January day in 2016 when my aunt knocked on the front door. When I answered the door, I suddenly felt my water break. My aunt drove me to the same hospital where, close to fifteen years before, I had given birth to my precious daughter, Cholie. We waited and waited, but the baby didn't come. After twenty-four hours, on January 5, they told me the baby was in distress and they needed to deliver by emergency C-section. He was a big baby and his head was in the 99th percentile for his size. He weighed eight pounds, thirteen ounces. After the nurse cleaned him up, she handed him to me, and I held in my arms my beautiful, chubby baby boy.

"I'd like to name him Deng, to honor my dad," I told Jordan, who readily agreed. *Deng* means "rain" in my Dinka language. My people, the Dinka, have alway depended on rain for feeding their cattle and growing food. Rain is seen as a blessing from God to all of creation, a common grace. And God had provided rain in my life.

Even when I didn't see the path clearly, God was still in control. He had answered the cry of my heart and opened doors for Jordan and me to return to Holland to be close to family. He had provided both of us with meaningful work—Jordan found a job with an inclusion consulting firm, and the American Bible Society allowed me to work offsite to continue with the Mission Trauma Healing program, formerly She's My Sister.

When I gave birth to Cholie, I was only a teenager and knew little about being a mom. Now I looked at this innocent baby, unscathed by war or suffering, and wondered what his life would be like. I was grateful that he and Cholie would never have to experience the trauma I had been exposed to. They are free, living in a free country, filled with opportunities to grow and to do great things with their lives. Yet as I cuddled this little one against my breast, safe in my arms, I thought about all the innocent children in war-torn countries who might never receive the kind of love and nurturing I was providing my children.

If there's one thing I've learned on this journey, it's that war never brings healing. The more people fight, the more trauma they produce, and it transfers from one generation to the next. That is not what I want for my children or for myself. My heart tells me that the answer is found only in divine love. Where there is love, there is peace. And peace brings restoration and new beginning for a healthy life. What brings healing is honoring the pain, acknowledging its impact, trusting God to secure lasting justice, and forgiving those who have caused our suffering. We must forgive others even though they may never seek forgiveness or say they are sorry for what they've done to us. I have waited for years to hear the word *sorry*, which has never come. When we refuse to forgive because we believe they must ask for it first, we allow ourselves to become a prisoner. Instead we forgive regardless of the other person, and then we find freedom.

I had to learn to forgive those who hurt me, and it's been a process. I had to hold my hands open and let God take that pain so I wouldn't become bitter. When we don't let those things go from our lives, freeing our minds and hearts, then we ultimately continue to give our power to the very people who harmed us.

But there's another aspect of forgiveness that we too often forget or neglect, and that is forgiving ourselves. If we want true forgiveness we must forgive ourselves for the ways in which we have failed ourselves. We do more damage to ourselves when we believe the lies others have said about us and the lies the enemy whispers into our minds— the lies that tell us we are no good, we are worthless, we can never experience true freedom or true love.

Don't do evil to yourself by listening or believing those voices of evil. Instead cling to these truths: God created you as a precious, unique, deeply loved and cherished human being. Nothing you can do—and nothing that has happened to you—can ever change that. God believes you

are priceless, and your wounds *do not* define who you are
in Jesus. If you have believed the lies and doubted these
truths, forgive yourself and embrace the precious gift
of you.

I cried for most of my childhood and early teenage
years. I was mad at God and couldn't understand all the
bad things he had allowed to happen. But one thing I
found to be true is that God hasn't given up on redeeming the world. Bad things happen, but the solution and the
redemption are embedded in the very problem. Knowing that, how could I harbor bitterness? Untreated heart
wounds fester and infect the soul and spirit. I chose the
path of hope, peace, and new beginning, and clung to
God's Word, which says, "They who wait for the LORD
shall renew their strength; they shall mount up with wings
like eagles; they shall run and not be weary; they shall walk
and not faint" (Isaiah 40:31).

I'd been a Lost Girl, traumatized, neglected, over-
looked, and yet God saw me. He didn't forget about me.
He reached down, redeemed my suffering, and said, *"You
are not without hope—ever—because I am with you."*

God placed me exactly where he wanted me to be to fulfill my purpose; he also gave me the desire of my heart: to
have good friends and a family—both Sudanese *and* American. Both have been instrumental in shaping me into the
person I have become. I want my life and my children's
lives to be strong; I want us to love God with all our hearts,
souls, minds, and strength; and I want us to give our lives

in grateful service to walking alongside people and making our world a better place.

There are still things I will never understand no matter how much education or experience I gain. At the top of that list is why bad things happen to innocent people, why innocent people suffer. Children, women, and men have died of wars they've never had a say over or involvement in. Why?

This is the question I have asked from a tender age. As I have grown older and seen the hand of God still at work in the world, I find myself nodding in agreement with Barbara Cawthorne Crafton, who said, "I am much less sure about most things than I used to be. But I feel the pull of the love of God all the time, and I don't care nearly so much about not understanding."

I guess that's why God calls each of us to a specific purpose—to serve others. Each of us is called to make this world a better place by addressing the issues of injustice. For me, sometimes that has been doing big-picture things—traveling to Africa to train leaders, telling my story to groups around the world, speaking with congresspeople on Capitol Hill on behalf of refugees and those whose voices are not heard, serving on the UN Refugee Congress and testifying about the plight of women and children who are seen as statistics, but who are living, breathing people whom God has seen and named and loves.

More often than not, however, serving others and

seeking justice is about doing the right thing for those around us. My foster family modeled this goodness when they stepped forward to help Cholie and me. Our lives are changed forever because of the goodness of others saying yes to a cause greater than themselves. That's what I want for my life and for the lives of my children.

Today my life is much different from what I could have ever imagined or hoped for when I was living at Kakuma Refugee Camp. My marriage is strong, and most of the South Sudanese community now praise Jordan, calling him a wonderful man who embodies many of the family values the Dinka hold dear. I am fulfilling my calling and I have a family I love, which now also includes my second daughter, Leona Nyandhot—named after Kokok—who was born on October 25, 2017. To invest in showing kindness and love to my family, in 2018 I took a break from work to be present for my kids. Though it is a sacrifice financially and career-wise, I am where I need to be.

As often as I can, I send financial aid to relatives still living in refugee camps all over East Africa. Many of my relatives are still living in refugee camps or war-torn areas and are struggling through their trauma. Recently I listened to and encouraged an aunt who went to jail because she became so depressed she started a fire in her condo. And when my half brother Luk was assaulted in Lansing, Michigan, and the doctors diagnosed him with a traumatic brain injury, Jordan and I took him in to live with us for several months. My half sister Nyanguom died of malnutrition and a treatable disease at a refugee camp in South

Sudan; she died in Atong's arms when Atong was only ten years old. I never saw Nyanguom again after we split up in Kapoeta. My half siblings Padiet, Atong, Angong, Nyandhot, and Madau now reside in Australia. Atong became a singer and songwriter, focusing on peace and unity for the South Sudanese people. Now as a single mother, however, she recently put her career on hold to focus on caring for her six children. I pray for and eagerly await the day we all can be reunited as a family.

A few years ago I reconnected with Mama Yar, who is still living in Kakuma with my last living paternal uncle and their children (she's been there since the camp's opening in 1992). She told me how difficult life is there now because the refugee camp is overcrowded and the rations are getting smaller and smaller. Education options have also become even more limited, as the refugee families are asked to pay school fees when they don't have jobs. And violence is still an issue between the different groups of refugees, as well as from citizens of their host country. She has been applying for resettlement for years, but continues to hear no word for her and her family.

Uncle Machok's widow—his second wife—now resides in Ontario with her four kids. And my cousin, who was born to Mama Adau, Uncle Machok's pregnant first wife— my aunt who got left behind in Bor when the UN vehicle we were on wouldn't wait for her to return from fetching water at the White Nile—is now in the army of South Sudan, although I haven't been able to track him down.

My family and I have suffered. And yet we are not alone

in that. Suffering is a universal language. I've seen over and over that we all share the same hurts, and when I speak with people and they share from their hearts, we sense Christ in our midst, knowing us in our suffering.

Although I have experienced healing, even after all these years, I still have moments when I grieve—something I know I will do for the rest of my life. There's no schedule for it. Something stirs up a memory and I go back to that place or time in my mind and I cry. Then I wipe my tears and move forward.

I grieve that I don't have many peaceful childhood stories to share with my children and future grandchildren. My deepest grief is that most of my relatives who died were not buried in a cemetery and there is no memorial I can visit. I pray and hope that one day I will be able to create a memorial for them. Most of my childhood stories are of suffering—war, starvation, and a lack of education. However, one story that is always true throughout my life is the story of love. Where there is love, all pain is overcome. Humanity's love is to feed the hungry, build schools, welcome refugees, and treat the sick. Humanity's love is to see people not as faceless, nameless ID numbers or statistics without stories. Jesus' love heals our wounded hearts and turns our pain into a beautiful learning journey.

That has been true for me. Though governments throughout the world still oppress their own people, I see cause for hope—that change starts with one person saying yes to God's call for peace and justice. I believe firmly that one person can affect another person and another—until war is no more, until children no longer have to fear a life without a mother and father, when villagers no longer have to flee their enemies. Peace can do those things. And God wants to do those things through each one of us.

🐿 🐿 🐿 🐿 🐿

For most of my life I have dealt with the question of who I am. Growing up, I knew I was a daughter of Deng Awel. I came from a family that had everything I could ever dream of—except my birth mother. I was raised by my grandmother, but most of my friends had their mothers and I knew I was different.

At Kakuma, I knew myself as a refugee totally dependent on the UN for food and at the mercy of the local Turkana people whose land we were residing on. I was a Sudanese girl. I was Dinka. I was an orphan.

When I came to the United States, I was still a refugee, but I became a foster child, an English as a Second Language student, an immigrant, a Lost Girl of Sudan, and an "alien." I became "naturalized," since, presumably, I was unnatural before, and then I became an American.

And I was lost. But God used a surprising source to show me my identity: my scars.

I used to be self-conscious about my feet and my legs, which still bear the scars of my escape from Sudan, as well as when I had night blindness from a lack of vitamins and

I walked straight into a tree and cut my left leg. These scars used to remind me about my hellish time; they were my source of shame. But slowly, as God healed my heart, I began to see my identity not as broken, but as beautiful. My scars were not a source of shame but of strength and resilience.

In the Bible, a young man named Joseph bore scars too. He had brothers who were extremely jealous of him, for Joseph was a gifted dreamer and their father's favorite. One day when they'd had enough of him, they threw Joseph in a well and sold him into slavery to a passing caravan heading to Egypt, never wanting to hear from him or see him again. Pleased to be rid of him, they told their father he was dead.

But God used what they had done to place Joseph exactly where God wanted him to be—in Egypt. And eventually Joseph became second in command in all of Egypt, managing a major food distribution program throughout a years-long famine. One day, who should show up for food but his brothers. And he told them, "You meant evil against me, but God meant it for good, to bring it about that many people should be kept alive" (Genesis 50:20).

That is my story. The soldiers and Sudanese government, my tribe's enemies and the man who took from me without knowing what true love is—they meant evil against me. But God meant it for good. Though Joseph's story is of an Israelite boy and mine is of a Dinka girl, our stories are the same in that they communicate the stories of suffering; but they also communicate that nothing is wasted in God's world. He redeems everything to himself. He uses people to restore justice and peace.

I am loved, deeply loved, and cherished by the Father of all good things. He is my protector, my identity, and my true home.

I am no longer a lost girl, for I have been found.

HOW YOU CAN GET INVOLVED

There is a great need, both internationally and domestically, to care for refugees. Though it is challenging work, we need to lift our heads to see them. If there is one thing my kokok could have done differently that dark day when I left my village, it would have been to lift her head to see me one more time. When I struggled through so much suffering, I cried, I curled up, I did everything that my broken heart wanted, but in the end I was able to lift my head. That is what refugees need—to have someone who will help them lift their heads in the midst of unspeakable injustice and suffering.

When I was growing up, my late uncle spent countless hours talking about the importance of a heart with sight. He argued that it is better for a person to have blind eyes than a blind heart. My preteen mind didn't understand this, but this changed in December 2009. After teaching afternoon classes, my favorite thing was taking a walk in the grasslands of Yabus in southern Blue Nile, Sudan. I saw this man who was completely blind, but was cutting trees to build his house.

He used his heart and hands to feel his chosen tree, avoiding thorns, termites, and rocks in his way. I sat and watched him for hours, as he felt each branch and stem and cut it without hurting himself. As we experience our world and its obstacles, and find ways to fix our world, may we lean more on heart-sight rather than depending only on eyesight!

You can visit www.rebeccadeng.com for more information about ways to get involved in providing support to refugees.

Acknowledgments

To Rachel and Lennis Baggech, thank you for giving me the chance to gain an education and for loving me and my daughter as your own.

To Teresa Nyaruach Wien, for true sisterhood we found in each other.

To Nyankai Clara Campbell, for being a wonderful college roommate and a great sister.

To my late father and mother, Deng Awel and Achol Riak, thank you for your legacy.

To my in-laws, Daniel and Janette Roeda, for loving me and accepting me as your daughter.

To Tim Beals, Ginger Kolbaba, and Keren Baltzer, for writing my story with me.

To Agot Aleer, for encouraging me years ago to write my story.

To Karen Genzink, for praying for and supporting me throughout the writing of this book.

To Megan Westlund, for helping resettle my aunt's family with her family. Thank you.

To Chuck and Julie Geenen, for your prayers, your faith, and your spiritual mentorship.

To my ESL teachers, Kathleen VanTol and Debra

Bandstra, and to my Bible teacher, Ray Vander Laan, for your insight, and for teaching me invaluable things.

To Uncle Dut Bethow, Deng Wuor Deng, Panchol Deng Ajang, Simon Luk, Aunt Monica Akuien, and Aunt Aker Riak, for their support all these years.

To Dr. Akech Koch, for his friendship during the 2011 referendum.

To Anyieth Dawol, for letting me rent a Dinka corset, and to the women at the Roots Project in Juba, South Sudan, for continuing our traditions of bead making.

No one realizes and fulfills their full potential on their own. Thanks to the wonderful men whom I dated and who affirmed in me that I am a woman clothed in strength and dignity. I am sorry for the immature ways I ended things in my relationships with you. The truth was that I was chained to my fears. To Tongwut, K-Maduk, M-Atong, and J, thank you for your respect and love.

To the nations that resettle and host refugees and to the men and women at the UN and other humanitarian agencies, for working on behalf of refugees.

To my best friend, Jordan Roeda, for helping me find the courage to say the two scariest words of my life: *I do*.

About the Authors

Rebecca Deng, of South Sudan's Dinka tribe, is one of the eighty-nine Lost Girls who came to the United States in 2000 as an unaccompanied refugee minor after living eight years in Kakuma Refugee Camp in northern Kenya. The violence she experienced as a child during the Second Sudanese Civil War (1983–2005) has given her a deep empathy for children and young adults who face similar situations today. She became a US citizen in 2006.

Today Rebecca is an international speaker and advocate for women and children who have been traumatized and victimized by war. She is a former Refugee Congress delegate at the United Nations High Commissioner for Refugees (UNHCR) in Washington, DC. She also led a team of referendum workers at one of the 2011 Out of the Country voting centers for the South Sudanese Independence Referendum. She worked with the American Bible Society's Mission Trauma Healing program, formerly called She's My Sister, for five years. In 2019, she and her family moved to Uganda, where her husband, Jordan, teaches community development in Mbale, while she continues to speak, travel, and consult.

Rebecca speaks Dinka and English, and understands Swahili and Arabic. She has a bachelor's in international development from Calvin College and a master's in ministry and organizational leadership from Grand Rapids

Theological Seminary. She studied in Thailand with International Sustainable Development Studies Institute and visited a refugee camp for Burmese families, after which she got her foster family's neighborhood involved in a project to sponsor hill-tribes-minorities refugees from that area.

She is married to Jordan Roeda and has three children, Cholie, Deng, and Leona. She resides with her family in Mbale, Uganda. She loves traveling, hiking, good conversation, and international cuisine.

Visit Rebecca at http://www.rebeccadeng.com, https://Facebook.com/RebeccaDengMedia, https://Instagram.com/rivkadeng, or https://twitter.com/rivkadeng.

Ginger Kolbaba is an award-winning author, editor, and speaker. She has written or contributed to more than thirty books, including *Breakthrough*, *Your Best Happily Ever After*, and *The Old Fashioned Way*. She is also a contributing editor for *Focus on the Family* magazine.

Ginger is the former editor of *Today's Christian Woman* magazine and *Marriage Partnership* magazine, and is the founding editor of Kyria.com, all award-winning resources of *Christianity Today*. In 2013, she started her own writing and editing business, in which she works with both major publishing houses and individuals.

Visit Ginger at http://www.gingerkolbaba.com, https://Facebook.com/GingerKolbabaAuthor, https://Instagram.com/gingerkolbaba, or https://twitter.com/gingerkolbaba.